W9-BXP-314

THE STORY
OF A SOUL

St. Thérèse of Lisieux
1873-1897
"The Little Flower"

THE STORY OF A SOUL

THE AUTOBIOGRAPHY OF SAINT THÉRÈSE OF LISIEUX

Edited by
Mother Agnes of Jesus

Translated by
Michael Day, CONG. ORAT.

TAN BOOKS AND PUBLISHERS, INC.
Rockford, Illinois 61105

NIHIL OBSTAT: GEORGIVS SMITH, S.T.D., PH.D.
CENSOR DEPVTATVS
IMPRIMATVR: E. MORROGH BERNARD
VICARIVS GENERALIS
WESTMONASTERII: DIE IX IVNII MCMLI

First published in 1951, by Burns Oates and Washbourne, Ltd. Retypeset and republished in 1997 by TAN Books and Publishers, Inc., by arrangement with Burns and Oates.

Library of Congress Catalog Card No.: 96-61307.

ISBN 0-89555-548-4

Cover illustration: St. Therese, portrait by her sister Celine (Sister Genevieve of the Holy Face). Photo: Helmuth Loose, from *Therese et Lisieux* by Descouvement and Loose. Reproduced by arrangement with Les Éditions du Cerf, Paris.

Frontispiece photo: Office Central de Lisieux.

Printed and bound in the United States of America.

TAN BOOKS AND PUBLISHERS, INC.
P.O. Box 424
Rockford, Illinois 61105
1997

"I feel that my mission is soon to begin, to make others love God as I do, to teach others my 'little way.' I will spend my Heaven in doing good upon earth . . ."

—St. Thérèse
July 17, 1897
(See page 213)

"The abundant fruits of salvation, remarkable and worldwide, that reading this so engrossing and touching work still daily produces, far exceed the results of efforts purely human."

—Decree on the Heroic Virtue
of Sister Thérèse
August 14, 1921

"The Sovereign Pontiff Pius X did not hesitate to declare that in this account of her life, which has now achieved a worldwide distribution, the virtues of the Maid of Lisieux shine so brightly that it is her very soul, as it were, that one breathes therein."

—Pope Pius XI
Brief of Beatification
April 28, 1923

CONTENTS

Foreword   ix
Translator's Note   xi
Prologue   xiii

For Mother Agnes of Jesus:

1. Early Childhood   1
2. At Les Buissonnets   16
3. Childhood Sufferings   33
4. Growing Up   46
5. Christmas Grace and After   64
6. Trip to Rome   84
7. Carmel   104
8. Profession and Oblation to
   Merciful Love   119

For Mother Marie de Gonzague:

9. Life in Carmel   138
10. The Way of Love   162

For Sister Marie of The Sacred Heart:

11. Immense Desires   191

Epilogue   207

FOREWORD

THE STORY OF A SOUL, better known to the English public as *The Autobiography of St. Thérèse of Lisieux*, was first published in 1899. Today it ranks with the greatest of the Church's spiritual classics, has been translated into practically every well-known language, and has had a worldwide influence. The reading of this book has brought innumerable people into the Church or back to the practice of their religion.

A wide experience over many years of the effect of this book upon souls shows quite clearly that *The Story of a Soul* possesses in some degree a characteristic common both to the *Gospels* and *The Imitation of Christ*. Men and women open the book, often quite casually, and are caught by the vivid clarity or simple profundity of some sentence in such a way that their lives are completely changed.

Clearly, the moment has come for *The Story of a Soul* to be published by itself, apart from other documents, so that it may speak for itself. This has been admirably achieved in the presentation of this new translation, which should bring home the message of St. Thérèse of Lisieux to many by whom it is not yet appreciated or understood.

VERNON JOHNSON

TRANSLATOR'S NOTE

THE following translation is made from the French edition of *L'Histoire d'une Ame* published from the Carmel of Lisieux for the fiftieth anniversary of the death of St. Thérèse de L'Enfant Jésus.

The manuscript is presented in its three original parts, while retaining the chapter divisions of the French edition. St. Thérèse's quotations from Scripture are closely interwoven with her text, and after great consideration the Douay translation was chosen as more easily reflecting the French she used.[1]

Italics, other than for Scripture quotations, are her own; diminutives and interjections, natural enough in the French but rarely used in English, have been omitted.

In the French, her style is extremely simple and spontaneous, having a charm which it is hard to capture, especially when she rises to poetic heights; it alters slightly in the three parts: the first eight chapters for Pauline are written without reserve; the two chapters for Mother Marie de Gonzague are more doctrinal and show a certain restraint; while the final chapter, for her eldest sister Marie, is simply a childlike outpouring of her heart to Jesus Himself.[2]

---

1. Scriptural references have been added to the text and enclosed in parentheses.—*Publisher*, 1996.
2. We have supplied chapter titles to make the text more readable.—*Publisher*, 1996.

I wish to express my gratitude to a religious of the Retreat of the Sacred Heart and to Miss Margaret Bacon for their generous help and advice and to all those whose co-operation has made this translation possible.

MICHAEL DAY
The Oratory, Edgbaston
*Feast of the
    Immaculate Conception*, 1950

PROLOGUE

LOUIS Joseph Stanislaus Martin was born on the 22nd of August, 1823, at Bordeaux, the son of the captain of the Garrison there. At the age of twenty, he sought admission to the Hospice of Mount Joux, the Great St. Bernard Hermitage in the Pennine Alps, but his entry was postponed.

At about the same time, Zélie Guérin, a lace-maker of Alençon in Normandy, attempted to join the Sisters of Charity, but she too returned home. When her sister entered the Visitation Convent at Le Mans she resolved on marriage, and prayed for many children, all of whom might be consecrated to God. On the 12th of July, 1858, she married Louis Martin, in the Church of Notre Dame at Alençon, and together they lived an exemplary Catholic life. Zélie's prayers were answered, for they had nine children. Four died at an early age, but of the rest, one entered the Visitation Convent at Caen, and the remaining four the Carmel at Lisieux.

Marie-Françoise Thérèse, their ninth child, was born at Alençon on the 2nd of January, 1873, after a series of prayers for a son. She was baptized two days later in the Church of Notre Dame, her eldest sister, Marie, being her godmother.

Four years later, her mother died, and the whole

family moved to Lisieux. It was there that she passed her childhood. At fifteen she became "Soeur Thérèse de L'Enfant Jésus" in the Carmel there, where she remained until her death at the age of twenty-four. She was canonized on May 17, 1925.

Her Autobiography was written under obedience, and it was only after her death that it was decided to let it pass beyond the walls of the Carmel.

It is interesting to note her views on the undesirability of a nun writing her memoirs. To one who expressed a wish to do so, she replied, "Mind you do nothing of the sort. You cannot do it without permission, and I advise you not to ask. For myself, I should not like to write anything about my life without an express order, and one which I had not solicited. It is more humble not to write anything about oneself. The great graces of one's life, such as one's vocation, cannot be forgotten. The memory of those graces will avail you more if you confine yourself to going over them in your mind, than if you write them down."[1] She used to tell her novices, "To have beautiful and holy thoughts and to write books or lives of the saints do not count so much as answering as soon as you are called."[2]

She showed reluctance when, in 1894, her second sister, Mother Agnes of Jesus, then Prioress, asked her to write down memories of her childhood. She began, however, at once, using a cheap exercise book, writing without plan or division, and only during the

---

1. *St. Teresa of Lisieux*, Henry Petitot, O.P., p. 134.
2. *Ibid.*, p. 119.

scanty free time allowed to Carmelites by their Rule. This first part of her Autobiography, begun towards the end of 1894, was completed on January 21, 1896, the Feast of St. Agnes.

Mother Marie de Gonzague, Prioress at the time of her entry, was re-elected that year, the year in which Sister Thérèse began to show signs of her fatal disease. At the request of Mother Agnes, she was told to complete her story; this time she wrote more slowly and very large, at times scarcely able to hold her pen, but still without method or revision. The last lines of this second part had to be written in pencil when she became too exhausted even to dip her pen in the ink-pot. This was in June and July of 1897.

Her eldest sister Marie, Marie of the Sacred Heart, had asked her the previous year to write something concerning her spirituality, and it was for her, again only under obedience, that she wrote the third part, a vindication of the value of supernatural love. This was in September of 1896.

The whole work was quite spontaneous; we may say that she did not so much write a book as live it, and then it wrote itself. Since its first publication, the appeal of the Autobiography has been universal, and the demand for it prodigious.

"The new St. Thérèse," said Pope Pius XI in the Homily of the Mass of Canonization, "was penetrated with the Gospel teaching, and put it into practice in her daily life. Yet more, she taught the way of spiritual childhood by her words and example to the novices of her Monastery, and she has revealed it to all by her writings, which have been spread all over

the world and which none can read without returning and re-reading them with great profit."

The Sacred Congregation of Rites in 1921 stated
that "in the Autobiography which Sister Thérèse
wrote by order of her Superiors we find a fact as
wonderful as it is universal, that is to say, the abundant fruit which is derived from the reading of this
attractive and fascinating biography—effects which far
exceed the narrow limits of the merely human.

"In fact this reading moves the hearts of men,
inclines their wills, amends their lives, kindles charity and produces other salutary results which
absolutely transcend human power, and can find no
adequate explanation except in the action of Divine
Grace itself."[3]

Of the rest, to the time of her death, she may
speak for herself.

---

3. The proclamation of the Heroic Virtue of Sister Thérèse of
   the Child Jesus by the Congregation of Rites, 14th August,
   1921.

THE STORY
OF A SOUL

Chapter 1

EARLY CHILDHOOD

MY dearest Mother, it is to you, to you who are in fact a mother twice over to me, that I now confide the Story of my Soul. The day you asked me to do it, I thought it might be a distraction to me, but afterwards, Jesus made me realize that simple obedience would please Him best. So I am going to begin singing what I shall sing forever, *"the mercies of the Lord."* (*Ps.* 88:1).

Before taking up my pen, I knelt before the statue of Mary, the one which has given us so many proofs that the Queen of Heaven watches over us as a mother. I begged her to guide my hand so that I should write only what would please her; then, opening the Gospels, my eyes fell on these words: *"Jesus, going up into a mountain, called unto Him whom He would Himself."* (*Mark* 3:13).

The mystery of my vocation, of my entire life, and above all, of the special graces Jesus has given me, stood revealed. He does not call those who are worthy, but those He chooses to call. As St. Paul says: *"God will have mercy on whom He will have mercy; so then it is not of him that willeth, nor of him that run-*

1

neth, but of God that showeth mercy." (Cf. *Rom.* 9:15-16).

For a long time I had wondered why God had preferences, why He did not give the same degree of grace to everyone. I was rather surprised that He should pour out such extraordinary graces on great sinners like St. Paul, St. Augustine and so many others, forcing His grace on them, so to speak. I was rather surprised, too, when reading the lives of the Saints, to find Our Lord treating certain privileged souls with the greatest tenderness from the cradle to the grave, removing all obstacles from their upward path to Him, and preserving the radiance of their baptismal robe from the stains of sin. Also, I wondered why so many poor savages die without even hearing Our Lord's name. Jesus chose to enlighten me on this mystery. He opened the book of nature before me, and I saw that every flower He has created has a beauty of its own, that the splendor of the rose and the lily's whiteness do not deprive the violet of its scent nor make less ravishing the daisy's charm. I saw that if every little flower wished to be a rose, Nature would lose her spring adornments, and the fields would be no longer enameled with their varied flowers.

So it is in the world of souls, the living garden of the Lord. It pleases Him to create great Saints, who may be compared with the lilies or the rose; but He has also created little ones, who must be content to be daisies or violets, nestling at His feet to delight His eyes when He should choose to look at them. The happier they are to be as He wills, the more perfect they are.

I saw something further: that Our Lord's love shines out just as much through a little soul who yields completely to His Grace as it does through the greatest. True love is shown in self-abasement, and if everyone were like the saintly doctors who adorn the Church, it would seem that God had not far enough to stoop when He came to them. But He has, in fact, created the child, who knows nothing and can only make feeble cries, and the poor savage, with only the Natural Law to guide him; and it is to hearts such as these that He stoops. What delights Him is the simplicity of these flowers of the field, and by stooping so low to them, He shows how infinitely great He is. Just as the sun shines equally on the cedar and the little flower, so the Divine Sun shines equally on everyone, great and small. Everything is ordered for their good, just as in nature the seasons are so ordered that the smallest daisy comes to bloom at its appointed time.

I expect you will be wondering, Mother, where all this is supposed to be leading, for so far I have not given you anything that looks much like my life-story—but you did tell me to write quite freely whatever came into my head! So you will not find my actual life in these pages so much as my thoughts on the graces Our Lord has given me.

I have reached the stage now where I can afford to look back; in the crucible of trials from within and without, my soul has been refined, and I can raise my head like a flower after a storm and see how the words of the Psalm have been fulfilled in my case: *"The Lord is my Shepherd and I shall want nothing.*

*He hath made me to lie in pastures green and pleasant;
He hath led me gently beside the waters; He hath led
my soul without fatigue . . . Yea, though I should go
down into the valley of the shadow of death, I will fear
no evil, for Thou, O Lord, art with me."* (Cf. *Ps.* 22:1,
4).

Yes, *"the Lord hath always been compassionate and
gentle with me, slow to punish and full of mercy."* (Cf.
Ps. 102:8). I feel really happy just to be able to tell
you, Mother, of all the wonderful things He has done
for me. Remember, I am writing for you alone the
story of the *little flower* gathered by Jesus, and so I
can speak unreservedly, not bothering about the style,
nor about the digressions I shall make; a mother's
heart always understands, even when her child can
do no more than lisp, so I am quite sure that you,
who prepared my heart and offered it to Jesus, will
certainly do so.

If a little flower could talk, it seems to me it would
say what God has done for it quite simply and without concealment. It would not try to be humble by
saying it was unattractive and without scent, that the
sun had destroyed its freshness or the wind its stem,
when all the time it knew it was quite the opposite.

This flower, in telling her story, is happy to make
known all the gifts that Jesus has given her. She knows
quite well that He could not have been attracted by
anything she had of her own. Purely out of mercy
He gave these gifts. It was He who caused her to be
born on soil which had been abundantly blessed,
where eight radiant lilies already bloomed, and where
the fragrance of purity was ever about her. In His

love, He wished to preserve her from the world's foul breath, and her petals were scarcely open when He transplanted her to the mountain of Carmel, to Mary's garden of delight.

Having told you so briefly what God has done for me, I will tell you in detail of my childhood. It may seem rather a dull story here and there, I know; but as you shared it all as I grew up at your side, as we shared the same saintly parents and together enjoyed their tenderness and care, I am sure it will not be without charm to your maternal heart.

I only hope they will bless their youngest child now and help her to sing the divine mercies.

The story of my soul before I entered Carmel can be divided into three definite periods. The first, though a short one, is rich in memories and extends from the dawn of reason to Mother's death—or in other words, until I was four years and eight months old. God graced me with intelligence at a very early age, and He so engraved the events of my childhood on my memory that it seems they happened only yesterday. Jesus wished, no doubt, that I should know and appreciate what a wonderful mother He had given to me, but sad to say, it was not long before His divine hand took her from me to be with Him in Heaven. He has surrounded me with love all my life; the first things I can remember are tender smiles and caresses, and while surrounding me with all this love, He gave me a warm and sensitive heart to respond to it. No one can imagine how I loved Father and Mother; I showed my affection for them in thousands of ways, for I was very demonstrative, and I

can't help smiling, even now, when I think of some
of the means which I used.

You let me keep the letters which Mother sent you
when you were a boarder at the Visitation Convent
of Le Mans. I remember quite clearly the incidents
they referred to, but it is much easier just to quote
certain passages of these charming letters. Dictated
by a mother's love, they are often far too flattering
to me. As an example of the way I used to show my
affection for my parents, take this letter of Mother's:

"Baby is such a little imp. In the midst of caress-
ing me, she wishes I were dead! 'Poor darling Mamma,
I do wish you were dead!' She is quite astonished
when I scold her, and excuses herself by saying, 'It's
only because then you will go to Heaven; you told
me that you have to die to go there!' In the same
way, she wishes her Father were dead, when her love
gets the better of her.

"The little darling never wants to leave me. She
always keeps close by me and loves to follow me
about, especially when I go out into the garden. She
refuses to stay when I am not there and cries so much
that she has to be brought in. Similarly, she will not
go upstairs by herself without calling to me at each
step, 'Mother! Mother!' As many 'Mothers' as there
are steps! And if by chance I forget to answer even
once, 'Yes, darling,' she stops just where she is and
won't go up or down."

I was almost three when she wrote:

"Little Thérèse asked me the other day if she is
going to Heaven. 'Yes, if you're good, Darling,' I
replied. 'If I am not,' she said, 'I suppose I shall go

to Hell. If so, I know what I will do. I will fly away to you, because you will be in Heaven—then you will hold me tight in your arms. God could not take me away then!' I could see by her face that she was quite sure God could not do anything to her if she were hidden in her mother's arms.

"Marie loves her little sister dearly. She is such a joy to all of us and so utterly sincere. It is charming to see her running after me to confess: 'Mother, I pushed Céline once, and smacked her once, but I won't do it again.'

"As soon as she has done the least thing wrong, everyone has to know about it. Yesterday, by accident, she tore a little corner off the wallpaper and got into a pitiful state. She wanted to tell her father about it as soon as possible. By the time he came home four hours later, everyone else had forgotten all about it, but she ran to Marie saying, 'Quick! Tell Father that I tore the paper.' She stood like a criminal awaiting sentence, but she had gotten the idea into her little head that he would forgive her more easily if she accused herself."

Father's name naturally brings back certain very happy memories. When he came home, I always used to run up to him and seat myself on one of his boots; he would then walk about with me like this wherever I wished, about the house and out in the garden. Mother used to laugh and say he would do whatever I wanted. "That is as it should be," he replied. "She is the queen." Then he used to take me in his arms, lift me up high to sit on his shoulder and make a tremendous fuss over me.

But I can't say he spoiled me. I remember one day very well. I was playing on the swing when he happened to be going by, and he called out to me: "Come and give me a kiss, my little queen." I did not want to move and—what was quite unlike me—answered mischievously, "You will have to come over here for it, Father!" He was wise enough to take no notice. Marie was there. "You naughty little thing," she said, "how can you be so rude to your father! Get off at once." I did get off my swing at once; I had really learned my lesson, and the whole house echoed with my cries of contrition. I ran upstairs and this time I did not call Mother at every step. I thought only of finding Father and making everything up, and that did not take very long.

I couldn't bear to think I had hurt my darling parents and used to admit my faults at once. The following account of Mother's will show how true this was: "One morning I wanted to kiss little Thérèse before going downstairs, but she seemed to be sound asleep, and I did not want to wake her up, until Marie said: 'Mother, I'm sure she is only pretending to be asleep.' I stooped down close to kiss her, but she hid herself under the sheet and said with the air of a spoiled child: 'I don't want anyone to see me.' I was far from being pleased, and let her know it. Not two minutes had gone by before I heard crying, and soon, to my surprise, there she was by me. She had gotten out of her bed by herself and stumbled all the way downstairs in her bare feet, wearing a nightgown far too long for her. Her little face was covered with tears, and burying her head in my lap, she cried: 'O Mother, I've been very bad; please forgive me.' She was forgiven at once. I took my little angel into my arms, held her to my heart and showered kisses on her."

I remember how very fond I was of my Godmother, who had just finished at the Visitation. Without showing it, I took in everything that was going on around me and all that was said; and I think I passed the same sort of judgment on things as I do now. I listened very carefully to everything she taught Céline and used to do whatever she told me, if only she would let me stay in the room while lessons were going on. In her turn, she was always giving me presents, and though they were not of much value, they gave me immense pleasure.

I was very proud of my two big sisters, but you seemed far away, so I used to dream of you from morning till night. When I was just beginning to talk, Mother used to ask me: "What are you thinking about?" and my answer was always the same, "Pauline." Sometimes I heard it said that you were going to be a nun, and without quite knowing what that meant, I said to myself: "I shall be a nun too." That is one of the first things I can remember, and I have never changed my mind since. So it was your example which drew me to the Spouse of Virgins when I was only two! I could tell you so much of what you have meant to me, Mother, only I am afraid I should never stop.

Darling Léonie had a big place in my heart too, and she loved me. When she came home from school in the evening, she used to take care of me while everyone else went for a walk. Even now I can almost hear the little songs she used to sing so sweetly to lull me to sleep. I can remember her First Communion very clearly, and I can remember her companion too; she was poor, and following the custom of the well-to-do families of Alençon, Mother had dressed her. This child did not leave Léonie's side for a moment that wonderful day, and at the grand dinner in the evening she was given the place of honor. I was too young to stay up, unfortunately, but I was not left out of the feast altogether, for Father, out of the goodness of his heart, came up to me during the dessert to bring his *little queen* a piece of the First Communion cake.

Last of all, I must tell you about Céline, who shared my childhood. I have so many memories of her that I do not know which to choose first. We both understood each other perfectly, but I was more lively and much less naïve than she was. Here is a letter which will remind you how good Céline was. It was when I was about three and Céline six and a half.

"Céline seems to be quite naturally good, but as for the other little monkey, I don't know what is to become of her, she is such a little madcap. She is intelligent enough, but not nearly so docile as her sister. When she says 'no,' nothing can make her change, and she can be terribly obstinate. You could keep her down in the cellar all day without getting a 'yes' out of her; she would rather sleep there."

I had one fault Mother does not mention in her letters. I was very proud, and here are only two examples of it:

One day, wishing to see just how far my pride would take me, she said to me laughingly: "If you will kiss the ground, Thérèse, I will give you a halfpenny." A halfpenny was a fortune to me in those days, and I did not have to stoop far to get it; I was so small that the ground was quite near. All the same, my pride was up in arms, and drawing myself up to my full height, I replied: "No, Mother! I'd rather go without the halfpenny." The other time was when we were going to visit some friends in the country. Mother told Marie to put on my nicest dress, but not to let me have my arms bare. I did not say a word and tried to seem as indifferent about it as I should have been at that age, but inwardly I was saying to myself: "Why? I should look so much prettier if I had my arms bare."

With tendencies like these, had I not been brought up by such wonderful parents, I am quite sure I should have gone from bad to worse and probably ended up by losing my soul. But Jesus was watching over His little bride and drew good even out of her faults, for as they were corrected very early, they helped her to grow more and more perfect.

I had a love for virtue, but I was proud too, so I only had to be told once: "You mustn't do that," and I never wanted to do it again. I am glad to see from Mother's letters that I became more of a consolation to her as I grew older. With only good example about me, it was only natural that I should tend to follow it. This is how she wrote in 1876: "Even Thérèse wants to start making sacrifices now. Marie has given each of the little ones a chaplet on which they can

keep count of their good deeds. They have real spiritual conferences together. It is most amusing. Céline
asked the other day: 'How can God get into such a
little Host?' Thérèse answered her: 'It's not surprising, since Our Lord is almighty.' 'What does almighty
mean?' 'It means He can do whatever he wants.' But
the most charming thing of all is to see Thérèse slip
her hand into her pocket time and time again and
move a bead along as she makes some sacrifice.

"These two children are inseparable and quite
happy to be alone together. Not so long ago, their
nurse gave Thérèse a small bantam cock and hen. She
gave the cock to her sister at once. After dinner every
evening Céline goes and catches the two birds, and
then they sit together in the corner of the fireplace
and play for hours. One morning, Thérèse decided
to climb out of her own little bed and go and sleep
in Céline's. When the maid, who was looking for her
to dress her, found her there, she put her arms around
her sister, and hugging her tight, said, 'Let me stay
here, Louise—can't you see we are just like the little
white chickens; we must always be together.'"

It was quite true; I could not bear to be parted
from Céline and would rather leave the table before
I had finished my dessert than let her go without me.
I would fidget about in my high chair, wanting to get
down at once, so that we could go and play together.

Because I was still too little to go to Sunday Mass,
Mother used to stay and look after me. I was very
good and quiet as a mouse, until I heard the door
open; then, simply bursting with joy, I rushed over
to my darling sister, saying, "Quickly, Céline! Give

me the blessed bread!" One day she had not brought any—what could be done? I could not go without it, for this little feast was my "Mass." I had a wonderful idea: "You haven't any blessed bread? Very well, then, make some!" She took the bread out of the cupboard and cut off a little piece; then having solemnly recited a Hail Mary over it, she presented it to me triumphantly. Making the Sign of the Cross, I ate it with great devotion and was quite sure it tasted like the real blessed bread. Another day, Léonie, who thought she had outgrown playing with dolls, came to look for us both, carrying a basketful of their dresses, little bits of material and other curiosities, with her doll laid on top. "Here, my dears," she said to us, "choose what you want." Céline examined them all and took a ball of silk braid. After a moment's thought, I put out my hand saying: "I choose everything," and carried off the basket, doll and all, without more ado.

I think this trait of my childhood characterizes the whole of my life; and when I began to think seriously of perfection, I knew that to become a Saint, one had to suffer much, always aim at perfection and forget oneself. I saw that one could be a Saint in varying degrees, for we are free to respond to Our Lord's invitation by doing much or little in our love for Him; to choose, that is, among the sacrifices He asks. Then, just as before, I cried: "I choose everything; my God, I do not want to be a Saint by halves. I am not afraid to suffer for Your sake; I only fear doing my own will, so I give it to You and choose everything You will."

But I am forgetting, Mother! I am supposed to be only three or four, and here I am talking about my adolescence!

I remember a dream I had at that age, which left a very deep impression: I was walking alone in the garden when suddenly I saw two horrible little devils near the arbor, dancing on a barrel of lime with amazing agility, in spite of having heavy irons on their feet. They looked at me with flaming eyes, then, as if overcome by fear, threw themselves in the twinkling of an eye to the bottom of the barrel. They escaped in some mysterious way and ran off to hide in the linen room, which opens onto the garden. When I saw how cowardly they were, I put my fears aside and went over to the window to see what they were up to. There the little wretches were, running round and round the table, and not knowing how to escape my gaze. From time to time they came nearer, still very agitated, to peep through the window; then, when they saw I was still there, they began racing about again in abject misery.

I do not suppose this dream was very extraordinary, but I do think God made use of it to show me that a soul in the state of grace need never be afraid of the devil, who is such a coward that even the gaze of a child will frighten him away.

I was so happy at this age, Mother, not only because I was beginning to enjoy life, but also because virtue had begun to appeal to me. I think my dispositions were the same then as they are now. I had acquired considerable self-control already, for I never complained when any of my things were taken away from me, and if ever I were unjustly accused, I would keep silent rather than excuse myself. There was no real virtue in this on my part, for it came naturally.

How swiftly these sunny years of childhood passed, yet what delightful memories they left behind! I love to think of the days Father used to take us to the pavilion, and most of all those Sunday walks, when Mother came with us. I can still feel the deep and poetic impression which the wheat fields made on me when I saw them all studded with poppies and corn-flowers and daisies. Even then I loved far distances, wide spaces and the trees. The whole of nature, in fact, enchanted me and raised my soul toward Heaven. During these long walks we often met poor people, and much to her delight, it was always little Thérèse who was sent to give them alms. On the other hand, much to her disgust, she was often taken home when Father thought the walk too long for his "little queen." However, Céline used to fill her little basket with daisies and bring them home to console her.

The whole world smiled on me; wherever I went my path was strewn with flowers, and my own happy nature helped to make life all the more delightful, but a new period was soon to begin. Since I was to become the Spouse of Jesus so young, I had to suffer from childhood. Spring flowers begin to grow beneath the snow before they open to the sun, and the little flower I am writing about had to pass through the winter of trial, and have her fragile calix watered with the dew of tears.

Chapter 2

AT LES BUISSONNETS

I CAN remember clearly all that happened when Mother was ill, and especially her last weeks on earth. Céline and I felt quite lost.

A friend used to come every morning to take us to her house for the day, and we left once without having time to say our prayers. On the way, Céline whispered: "Do we have to tell her we haven't said our prayers yet?"

"Of course we must," I replied.

So Céline very shyly told her about it when we arrived. "You shall say them then, my dears," she replied, and putting us in a large room, she left us to ourselves. Céline turned to me in astonishment, and I was surprised too. "Mother's not like that," I exclaimed; "she always says our prayers with us."

We couldn't think of anyone else but Mother all day, though they made every effort to keep us amused. Céline, I remember, was given a lovely apricot. She leaned toward me and whispered, "Let's not eat it, but keep it for Mother." How sad! Darling Mother was far too ill to enjoy such earthly fruits; only the blessedness of Heaven could satisfy her now, where she would drink that mystic wine which, at the Last Supper, Jesus said He would share with us in His Father's Kingdom.

The moving ceremony of Extreme Unction impressed me very much; I remember just where I knelt, and I can still hear Father weeping.

The day after Mother died, he lifted me into his arms and said: "Here, my little one, kiss your darling Mother for the last time." Silently, I touched her cold forehead with my lips. I do not think I cried very much, and I told no one of all that was going on inside me. Without saying anything, I just watched and listened and saw a lot that they wanted to keep from me. On one occasion, I was all alone near the coffin, which was left standing on its end in the corridor. I stood there, deep in thought, for ages. It was the first time I had seen one, but I knew what it meant well enough. As I was so little, I could not see all of it without raising my head. How big and gloomy it seemed!

Fifteen years later, I found myself in front of another coffin, this time, that of our saintly Mother Genevieve, and it all came back to me. It was the same Thérèse, but grown up now, and this coffin did not look big at all. She did not have to raise her head, save toward Heaven, where all her happiness was placed, experience having so matured her soul that nothing on earth could sadden her any more.

The day the Church blessed Mother's mortal remains, God did not leave me quite an orphan; He let me choose another mother for myself. We were all together, I remember, the five of us, looking sadly at one another, and nurse turned to Céline and me, deeply touched at our misery, saying: "Poor darlings, you haven't got a mother any more!" Céline threw herself at once into Marie's arms, saying: "Then you shall be my mother now." As I always used to do the same as Céline, I might have followed her example in this, only I thought you might be rather hurt and feel you had been left out if you did not have a little daughter too. So I looked lovingly at you and buried my head in your breast, saying in my turn: "Pauline's going to be *my* Mother!"

It was now, as I have mentioned, that the second and saddest stage of my life was to begin, especially after you, my second mother, entered Carmel. This period lasted from the time I was four and a half until I was fourteen; it was only then that I got back the gaiety of my earlier days, though with it there came a growing realization of the seriousness of life.

You remember, I am sure, how all my gaiety went after Mother died. I had been so lively and open; now I became diffident and over-sensitive, crying if anyone looked at me. I wanted to be left alone and hated meeting strangers. It was only in the intimacy of my own family, where everyone was wonderfully kind, that I could be more myself. Father's heart, which was affectionate enough already, seemed to become infinitely loving, and both you and Marie were the kindest and most unselfish of mothers to me. If God had not poured out His light so lavishly upon His "little flower," she could never have become acclimatized to earth, for she would have been too frail to weather the rain and storm; she had to have warmth and gentle dew and the soft breezes of spring, and even in the winter of trial these never failed her.

It did not make me sad to leave Alençon. Like all children, I loved change and things out of the ordinary, so I enjoyed moving to Lisieux. I remember the journey well. We arrived at our uncle's house in the evening, and Jeanne and Marie and Aunt were standing at the door waiting for us. I was very moved by all the love they showed us. We were taken to Les Buissonnets, our new home, the next day. It was in a quiet part of the town and not far from the Jardin de l'Etoile with its lovely flowered walks.

I was quite charmed by the house, and my imagination was carried away by the distant view from the belvedere, the trim gardens at the front of the house and the larger garden at the back. This lovely house was to be the setting for so many delightful times for all of us. Everywhere else I felt lost and used to cry and miss Mother, but there my little heart opened out, and I could greet life with a smile.

You were always there to kiss me awake, and I said my prayers kneeling beside you. Then you used to give me a reading lesson. The first word I could read by myself, I remember, was "Heaven." When this was over, I used to go upstairs to the belvedere, where Father spent most of his time, wonderfully happy if I could tell him I had had good marks.

He used to take me for a little walk every afternoon to pay a visit to the Blessed Sacrament in the various churches in turn. It was then that I saw the Carmel chapel for the first time. "Look, my Little Queen," said Father, "there are holy nuns behind that big grille, always praying to God." It certainly never occurred to me that I would be among them before nine years were gone, that there, in this Carmel, I was to have many graces poured out on me.

When we got home from our walk, I used to finish my lessons and then spend the rest of the day romping around Father in the garden. I was never very interested in playing with dolls, but I really used to enjoy making strange concoctions from seeds and the bark of trees. When these came out with an attractive color, I used to pour some into a pretty, tempting little cup and invite Father to try it. He would stop what he was doing and, smiling all the time, pretend to drink.

I used to love growing flowers, and making little altars too, in a niche which I had been lucky enough to find in the garden wall. When I had finished decorating them, I used to run and fetch Father, and he would come and stand enraptured before my masterpiece of an altar, just to please me. I can remember thousands of things like that, but if I were to tell you about them, I would never finish; in any case no words can express the tenderness our incomparable father lavished on his little queen.

What lovely days those were for me when my "king," as I loved to call him, used to take me with him when he went fishing. I used to try to fish sometimes myself, with my own little rod, but usually I preferred just sitting a little way off in the flowery grass. My thoughts used to become very deep then, and though I had no idea of what meditation was, my soul was really lost in prayer. I listened to the sounds that came from far away and the murmur of the wind. Sometimes snatches of martial music were carried from the town, making me feel rather sad; earth seemed to me a place of exile, and I dreamed of Heaven.

Such afternoons passed quickly, and it was soon time to return home to Les Buissonnets, but before gathering all our things together, I used to eat the food I had brought in my basket. Even the lovely jam sandwiches you had made for me looked different now. The jam had lost its rich color, gone a miserable pink and sunk into the bread. This made the earth seem a sadder place than ever, and I was quite convinced that one would never find unclouded happiness this side of Heaven!

Speaking of clouds, there was one day I remember when there was nothing but lovely blue sky over the countryside; then far away there was the rumble of thunder and flashes of lightning. I looked all round, not wanting to miss any of this awe-inspiring sight and was not the slightest bit frightened but quite delighted when I saw a thunderbolt fall in a nearby meadow. God seemed very near. Father was not so happy about it as his queen and brought my enchantment to an end very quickly, for there were several fields between us and the road, and already the grass and the huge daisies, taller even than I was, were glistening with jewels.

He carried me in his arms, in spite of the fact that he was carrying his fishing tackle too, and from this vantage point, I looked down upon the lovely diamonds, almost sad that I, too, was not adorned with them.

So far I have not said anything about how I often gave alms to the poor people we met on those daily walks we used to go on in Lisieux and Alençon.

There was one poor old man on crutches we met, dragging himself along with difficulty. I went up to him and offered him my penny, but he simply looked at me very sadly, shook his head, and with a wry smile, refused it. I had only wanted to do what I could for him, and yet I had perhaps hurt and humiliated him. You have no idea what I felt like!

When we had gone on some way, however, I saw him turn about and smile at me, so he must have guessed what had been going on in my mind.

As Father had just bought me a cake, I felt a great desire to run and give it to the old man, saying to myself: "He will not take any money, but I am sure he would like a cake," but for some reason I was too frightened to do this, and I felt so miserable about it that I almost cried. At that moment, I remembered someone saying that everything we asked for on the day of our First Communion would be granted, and I felt happy again. I was only six then, but I made up my mind that I would pray for this poor man on that day, and five years later I kept my resolution. I am quite sure that Our Lord heard and answered my prayer for this suffering member of His.

I came to love God more and more as I grew up and often offered my heart to Him in the words Mother had taught me. I used to try hard to please Jesus in everything I did and never offend Him. There was one day, however, when I committed a fault which is well worth telling you about; I think I have had perfect contrition for it, but it will be a chance of humbling myself.

It was in May, 1878. As you thought I was still too young to go to May Devotions, I used to stay at home with the nurse and make mine in front of my own little altar, which I had arranged myself with candlesticks and vases of flowers. It was all on such a small scale, candlesticks included, that it could be lit up with only two matches as candles. As a surprise on rare occasions, Victoire would let me have two stumps of real candle to save my own. One evening, as we were about to pray, I asked her to say the "Memorare" while I lighted the candles; she made as if to begin, looked at me and then burst out laughing. Seeing my precious matches burning out, I begged her again to say the "Memorare" at once. All I got was silence and then another burst of laughter. Filled with indignation, I got up, stamped my foot hard and shouted at her, "You wicked Victoire!"

The poor girl did not feel like laughing any more and simply looked at me, silent with astonishment, then showed me, all too late, the surprise she had wanted to give me; two beautiful pieces of candle she was hiding under her apron! I cried as much in my remorse now as I had in my anger and was so ashamed of myself that I made up my mind it would never happen again.

I made my first Confession not long after this. I remember your saying to me: "You are not going to confess your sins to a man, my Darling, but to God Himself," and I took this so to heart that I asked you quite seriously if I should not tell Father Ducellier that I loved him with all my heart, since it was really God I was going to speak to.

I had been taught exactly what I had to do, and I went into the confessional and knelt down, but when the priest opened the shutter, he could not see anyone because I was so small my head was hidden by the armrest. He told me to stand up, and I did so at once; turning round so that I could just see him, I made my confession. I made a big act of faith when I received my absolution, since you had told me it was at this most solemn moment that my soul would be purified by the tears of the Child Jesus. I remember the direction he gave me: he urged me above all to have great devotion to Our Lady; she already occupied a very large place in my heart, but I promised to give her even more. I gave him my rosary to bless and then left the confessional with such a light heart that I think I had never been so happy before. It was getting dark. I stopped under the first street lamp and pulled my newly blessed beads out of my pocket; then I began to subject them to a very careful examination.

"What are you doing, Thérèse?" you asked me.

"Trying to see what a blessed rosary looks like," I answered. My naïve reply caused you tremendous amusement.

The grace I received then had a lasting effect on me, and I went again every big feast day; and every time, my confession gave me a foretaste of eternal happiness.

Feast days! Those words conjure up more wonderful memories! I did so love them and you were able to explain so well what they were all about. That again was a foretaste of Heaven. But the procession of the Blessed Sacrament was what I loved best, for I could scatter flowers beneath the feet of God! I used to throw them up high into the air before they fell and when my rose petals touched the monstrance my happiness was complete.

The big feasts did not come along so often but there was one most dear to me, and it came every week—Sunday, Our Lord's own day, a wonderful day, a day of rest.

We all went to the High Mass, and when it was time for the sermon, I remember we had to leave our place because it was so far away from the pulpit and go all up the nave to find places nearer. This was not always easy to do, but everyone seemed quite ready to find room for little Thérèse and her father. Uncle, especially, seemed very happy when he saw us coming; he used to call me his little ray of sunshine and say that the sight of this venerable patriarch hand in hand with his little daughter always touched his heart.

The fact that all this drew attention to us never bothered me; I was far too interested in what the priest was saying.

The first sermon I really understood was one on Our Lord's Passion, and I was very much moved by it; that was when I was five and a half, and from then on I could take in and appreciate all that was said.

If ever St. Teresa was mentioned, Father used to bend down toward me and whisper: "Listen, my Little Queen, he is talking about your Patron Saint."

Then I would really listen, but I am afraid I kept my eyes on Father far more than on the preacher because I could read such a lot in his noble face. Sometimes his eyes would fill with tears he could not keep back, and when he was listening to the eternal truths, he seemed to be already in another world and no longer in this. He was then a long way from his journey's end, however; long, sad years had yet to pass before he opened his eyes on Heaven's loveliness and Jesus wiped away His faithful servant's tears. But to come back to my Sundays: these wonderful feasts, which used to pass so swiftly, were not untinged with sadness, and after Compline my happiness gave way to a certain pensiveness.

Tomorrow I would have to go back again to my daily routine and my lessons; I felt an exile again and longed for Heaven, my true home, where it would be always Sunday.

We used to take turns spending our Sunday evenings with our aunt before going home to Les Buissonnets, and I used to look forward so much to my turn. I used to love listening to everything Uncle talked about, especially when he was being serious; I am sure he never guessed how interested I really was. I was not too happy, however, when he used to sit me on his knee and sing me a song called "Blue Beard"; his voice was rather formidable!

Father would come and fetch me about eight o'clock. I remember how I used to love looking up at the stars on the way home. I was quite fascinated by Orion's Belt, which hung like a cluster of golden pearls across the deep vault of the sky, for they seemed to me to form the letter "T." "Look, Father," I used to say, *my name is written in Heaven*." Then this miserable earth lost all interest for me, and I would ask him to guide me; without looking where my feet were going, I threw my head back and never tired of gazing at the stars.

During the winter evenings at Les Buissonnets we used to play draughts; then the board was whisked away, and you or Marie would read out loud to us some of the *Liturgical Year*, followed by a few pages from some other good and fascinating book. All this time, I would be perched on Father's knee, and when it was over, he used to sing most beautifully some lullaby while he rocked me to sleep, pressing me gently to his heart.

At long last we would all make our way upstairs to say our night prayers, and once again I would find myself close to him, only having to look at him to know how Saints must pray.

After you had tucked me into bed, I always used to ask you: "Have I been good today? Do you think God is pleased with me? Will the little Angels come and shield me with their wings?" I always got the answer, "Yes." I would have cried all night otherwise. After all that, you and Marie would kiss me goodnight; then little Thérèse was left alone in the dark. I count it very fortunate that I was taught at this early age to overcome my fear of the dark. You often used to send me by myself at night to fetch things from a room on the other side of the house, never allowing me to get out of going; it was really good for me because I was far too timid. Now it is very hard to frighten me.

It is a wonder to me how you managed to bring me up so lovingly without spoiling me, but you certainly did. You never let me off with a single little fault and never went back on any decision you had made, though you never rebuked me unless there was good reason.

I used to tell you my most secret thoughts, and you would set at rest any childish doubts I had.

I told you once how it puzzled me that God did not give everyone the same amount of glory in Heaven, and I feared they could not all be happy. You sent me off to fetch one of Father's big glasses and made me put my little thimble by the side of it; then you filled them both up with water and asked me which I thought was the fuller. I had to admit that one was just as full as the other because neither of them would hold any more.

That was the way you helped me to grasp how it was that in Heaven the least have no cause to envy the greatest.

By explaining such great mysteries in a way I could understand, you gave my soul its necessary food.

Prize-giving every year! Though I was the only competitor, this did not mean that I was let off easily; I was never given a prize unless I had really deserved it. How my heart used to beat when my report was read out in the presence of the whole family or when I went up to have my prizes presented by my "king." I used to think the Day of Judgment must be just like that. I had no suspicion of what Father was to go through then, because he always seemed so cheerful, until God lifted the veil over the future in a strange vision. Father had gone on a journey and was not due back until late. At about two or three o'clock, I think, when the afternoon sun was shining and nature was at its best, I happened to be standing all alone, my mind full of delightful thoughts, at a window overlooking the garden at the back.

Then, across the garden by the wash-house, I saw a man dressed exactly like Father, the same height and the same walk, only much older and with a stoop.

I say he looked older, but this was only the impression I got. I could not see his face because it was heavily veiled. Slowly, deliberately, he came toward me; he passed my own little plot of garden; and then a strange fear crept over me; I began to cry out, my voice trembling, "Father! Father!" He did not seem to hear, did not even turn around, but passed straight on toward the group of fir trees which divided in two the main path of the garden. I waited, expecting him to reappear on the other side of the trees, but the prophetic vision was gone.

This all took place in a short space of time, but it made such a vivid impression on me that the memory of it is just as real to me as the vision itself.

Marie was with you in a nearby room, and the way I was calling "Father" frightened you both. Marie ran in to me, trying to hide her feelings, and said: "Why are you calling Father like that when he is in Alençon?" I explained what I had seen, and to reassure me, you told me it must have been the maid who had drawn her apron up over her head to try to scare me. When Victoire was asked about it, however, she swore she had never left the kitchen. It did

not make any difference anyway because I was convinced in my own mind: I had seen a man, a man
exactly like Father.

We went out and looked behind the clump of trees,
but there was nothing there. Then you told me to
think no more about it, but how could I do that? This
strange vision kept coming back to me, and I often
tried to lift the veil which hid its secret, while in my
heart I was sure it would be lifted entirely one day.

You know all the rest now; you know that it really
was Father whom God allowed me to see coming
toward me, bent with age and with the symbol of
his dreadful trial upon his venerable white head. As
the adorable face of Jesus was veiled during His Passion, it was only fitting that the face of His faithful servant should be veiled during his time of
humiliation and so in Heaven shine with all the
greater radiance.

I am full of wonder at God's ways. A father loves
to share with his children the joyful anticipation of
the future he is planning and of their rich inheri-
tance, and so God let us catch a glimpse of this precious cross to come.

It did puzzle me, nevertheless, why He should give
this vision to a child who would have died of sorrow
if she had understood. It is one of those unfathomable
mysteries which we will understand only in Heaven;
then our wonder will know no bounds. O God, how
good Thou art to temper every trial to our strength.
At that time I had so little courage that the very
thought of losing Father would have terrified me.

One day when he had climbed to the top of a ladder and I was standing rather near, he called down: "Move out of the way, my Little Queen; if I fall down I shall crush you."

My heart revolted at the idea, and I came even closer, saying to myself: "If he falls down, I will not have the grief of seeing him die; I shall die too."

I cannot tell you how much I loved him, and I admired him in everything he did. When he used to expound to me some of his ideas on serious matters, as though I were already grown up, I would tell him in all simplicity: "If you talked that way to the great men in the government, they would make you King for certain; then France would be happier than ever before.

"The trouble is, you would be miserable, because kings always are, and also you would not be my very own King, so I am glad they do not know you."

I saw the sea for the first time when I was about six or seven, and the sight impressed me so much I could not turn my eyes away.

It was so majestic! And the voice of the waves spoke to my soul of God's power and grandeur.

I remember a man and his wife on the beach asking Father if I belonged to him and saying I was very beautiful. I felt rather pleased at hearing this because I had not thought I was, but Father stopped them from paying me any more compliments.

As you had always taken great care to say nothing which might destroy my childlike simplicity and I thought no end of you, I attached little value to their admiring words and glances and thought no more about the matter.

That same evening, when the sun appeared to be sinking into the vast stretch of the waters beyond a golden path of light, I went with you to sit upon a lonely rock. I gazed for ages on this path of light, and you said it was an image of the path to Heaven when grace lights up the way.

Then I thought of my heart as a tiny ship with white and graceful sails gliding down the middle of a path of gold, and I resolved that I would never sail it out of sight of Jesus, so that it might voyage swiftly and in peace toward the shores of Heaven.

Chapter 3

CHILDHOOD SUFFERINGS

WHEN I was eight and a half, Léonie left the Abbey and I took her place. I was put in a class of girls all older than myself, and among them was one of fourteen, who was not very clever but able to dominate the others. Jealous at seeing me, young as I was, nearly always at the top of the class and a favorite with all the nuns, she found a thousand ways to pay me back for my little victories. As I was naturally rather reserved and sensitive, I did not know how to defend myself. All I could do was to cry and say nothing about it. You, Mother, and Céline did not know how unhappy I was. I was not virtuous enough to rise above all this, and so my heart suffered very much.

Fortunately, I could go home every evening, and then I cheered up. I used to jump on Father's knee and tell him what marks I had had, and when he kissed me, all my troubles were forgotten. How happy I was when I was able to tell him I had gotten full marks for my composition. He gave me a bright little silver coin as a reward. I put it in my money box for the poor and used to add to it every Thursday.

I needed this sort of encouragement so much; the "little flower" had to thrust its tender roots deep down into the specially prepared soil of its beloved home, because only there could it find its necessary food. Thursday was always a half-holiday in school. It was not at all like the holidays you used to give me at home, which I usually spent with Father on the terrace. I did not know how to play like the other children, and I was not much fun for them, but I did do my best to join in, even though it was never any good. I could not get on without Céline, but next to her, my little cousin Marie was my favorite because she always let me choose my games. We thought about and loved the same sort of things. It was as if God were preparing us, even then, for the day when both of us would be in Carmel.

At Uncle's house, Marie and I often used to pretend we were penitent anchorites with nothing but a poor hovel, a tiny cornfield and a garden for a few vegetables. Our life was spent in continual contemplation, or rather one of us used to pray while the other was busy with more material things. We did everything silently, in perfect harmony with each other, and we behaved as good religious should. When we went out for a walk, we kept up this game, even in the street. The two hermits would say the Rosary, but on their fingers, so that they should not betray their devotions in public, but one day, Thérèse the recluse forgot. She had been given a cake for her lunch, and before eating it, she made a big Sign of the Cross; some of the more worldly could not help smiling. Sometimes we went too far in trying to copy each other. One evening, coming home from the Abbey, we tried to imitate the modesty of hermits. I said to Marie: "You lead me, I am going to shut my eyes." "I want to shut mine too," she replied, so we both did what we wanted to. As we were walking on the pavement, we did not have to worry about the traffic, but after a few minutes, thoroughly enjoying walking with closed eyes, the two scatterbrains fell over some packing-cases standing at the door of a shop and knocked them over. The shopkeeper was very cross and rushed out at once to rescue his goods. The would-be blind picked themselves up and hurried off with their eyes and ears wide open to get a well-deserved scolding from Jeanne, who seemed just as cross as the shopkeeper.

I have said nothing so far of how my relations with Céline altered. At Lisieux our rôles were completely changed: she was now the mischievous imp, and Thérèse the quiet little girl who cried too much. She needed someone to stand up for her, and I can't tell you how bravely her darling little sister took on the part. We often exchanged little gifts, which gave us both tremendous delight. How unsophisticated we were at this age; our souls opened out in all their freshness like the spring flowers happy to receive the dew at dawn, our petals swaying to the same light breeze. We shared all our joys, and I felt that very strongly on the wonderful day of Céline's First Communion, when I was only seven and had not yet started at the Abbey. What lovely memories I have of her preparation! During the last few weeks, you used to talk to her every evening about the great step

she was going to take; I used to listen too, eager to
prepare myself, and when told to go away because I
was still too young, how sad I was. Surely, I thought,
four years was not too long to spend preparing to
receive Our Lord.

One evening I overheard you saying to my sister:
"After your First Communion, you must begin an
entirely new life." I made up my mind at once that
I would not wait until my Communion before starting this new life, but would begin when she did.

During her retreat, she stayed at the Abbey, and
the time passed very slowly for me, until at last the
great day came. It made a wonderful impression on
my heart and seemed like the prelude to my own
First Communion; I received such graces that day
and look back on it as one of the loveliest of my life.

I have rather interrupted my story by going back
to this delightful memory, so now I must go on to
speak of the time when Jesus took from me the "little mother" I loved so much. This separation nearly
broke my heart. I remember that I said once that I
should like to go with you to a far-off desert, and
you said that you felt the same, but would wait until
I was big enough. Little Thérèse had taken this
impossible promise seriously, and it hurt dreadfully
to hear her dear Pauline talking to Marie about entering Carmel soon. I did not know what Carmel was;
I only knew she was going to enter a convent and
leave me; she was not going to wait for me.

How can I describe what went on in my heart? In
a moment I saw what life is really like, full of suffering and continual separations, and I burst into bit-

ter tears. I did not know then the joy of sacrifice; I was weak, so weak that I look upon it as a great grace to have been able to bear a trial which seemed quite beyond me.

I shall always remember how tenderly my little mother consoled me. She told me what life in the cloister was like, and one evening later on, when I was all alone turning these things over in my mind and thinking about the picture she had drawn for me, I felt that Carmel was the desert in which God wished to hide me too. I felt this so intensely that there could be no doubt about it. This was no childish dream nor the enthusiasm of a moment. It had about it the certainty of a divine call, and this indescribable feeling was accompanied by deep peace.

Next day I told you of my desires. You believed they were from Heaven and promised you would take me soon to Carmel to tell my secret to Mother Prioress.

A Sunday was chosen for this solemn visit. I was rather embarrassed to find that my cousin Marie, still young enough to see the Carmelites face to face, was to come with me. I had to think of some way of being left in the parlor alone, and this is what I decided to do: I told Marie that, as it was such a privilege to see Reverend Mother, we ought to be very good, and that the polite thing to do would be for each of us to confide in her; that would obviously mean that first one, then the other would have to go out for a while.

Marie was not very happy about it as she hadn't anything to confide anyway, but she accepted what

I said, and I was able to have my private talk with
Mother Marie de Gonzague. She listened as I told
her my secret and said she thought I had a vocation
but that they did not receive postulants who were
only nine; I should have to wait until I was sixteen.
I had to be content with just making my First Communion on the day you took the veil, instead of entering with you, as I longed so much to do.

The second of October came as a day of tears and
blessings as Jesus gathered the first of His flowers,
the chosen one who was to become a few years later
the Mother of her sisters. While Father, with Uncle
and Marie, climbed Mount Carmel to offer his first
sacrifice, my aunt took me to Mass with Léonie and
Céline. We were crying so much when we went into
church that everyone looked at us in surprise, but
this did not stop us. I wondered how the sun could
go on shining.

Dear Mother, you probably think I am exaggerating, and I quite see that saying good-bye to you
should not have upset me so much. But I really was
still something of a baby and had to go through many
a storm before I reached the harbor of peace or tasted
the fruits of total surrender and perfect love.

That afternoon, I saw my dear Pauline behind the
grille of Carmel as Sister Agnes of Jesus. How I suffered on that visit. As I am writing the story of my
soul, I think I should put down everything, so I must
tell you that this first pain of being separated seemed
as nothing compared with what followed. I was used
to having heart-to-heart talks with my little mother
whenever I wanted. Now I could only get a few

moments when the family had finished, and even that
was not easy. Of course I spent those few minutes
crying and went away heartbroken. I didn't understand that it would have been impossible to give us
half an hour each, and that naturally most of the time
belonged by right to Father and Marie. I did not
understand, and deep down in my heart I thought,
"I have lost Pauline." The weight of this suffering
caused my mind to develop much too quickly, and it
was not long before I was seriously ill.

There is no doubt that the devil had a hand in
this illness; he was probably so jealous over your entry
into Carmel and all we were going to do against him
in the time to come that he wanted to vent his fury
on me. He did not know that the Queen of Heaven
was keeping faithful watch over her little flower, smiling down on her from above. She was ready to calm
the storm just when the frail and slender stem was
in danger of being broken forever.

At the end of the year 1882, I developed a continual headache, which went on until Easter 1883.
It was just bearable and did not stop me going on
with my studies. About that time Father went to Paris
with Marie and Léonie, leaving Céline and me in the
care of my uncle and aunt.

One evening, when I found myself alone with my
uncle, he talked about Mother and of the past so tenderly that it touched me deeply and made me cry;
he was most moved to find me so sensitive, and was
so surprised to find that I could feel as I did, that
he made up his mind to do all he could during the
holidays to turn my mind on to other things.

But God chose otherwise: That very evening, my headache developed most violently, and I was seized with a strange trembling, which went on all night. My aunt, like a true mother, did not leave me for a moment, and all through my illness she was wonderfully tender, looking after me with most devoted and delicate care.

I can't describe what Father went through when he got back from Paris and found me so ill. Before long, he became convinced that I was going to die, but Our Lord would have told him: "*This sickness is not unto death, but for the glory of God.*" (*John* 11:4).

Yes, the end of this trial really was the glory of God! He was glorified by the wonderful resignation of my father, and of my sisters, and especially of Marie. How she suffered, and what a great debt I owe her! Her heart told her what to do, and the insight of the most skilled doctors can't compare with that of a mother's heart.

All the while, Mother, the day when you were to take the habit was drawing nearer. No one talked about it in front of me, for fear of causing fresh trouble, for they were all quite convinced I would not be able to go. But deep in my own heart, I was sure that God would console me by letting me see you again on that day—that the feast day would be cloudless. Surely Jesus would not give pain to His bride, by leaving me out; my illness had caused you enough suffering already. I was not mistaken; in fact, I was able to put my arms around you, sit on your knee, hide myself underneath your veil and receive your loving caress. I was able to gaze at you for a moment, looking so lovely in your snow white veil. It was a wonderful day, breaking in upon my time of darkness; but that day, or rather that short hour, passed all too quickly, and soon I had to return to the carriage, which took me away from you.

When I got back to Les Buissonnets, they sent me to bed, though I did not feel the slightest bit tired. The next day, however, I had a bad relapse, and the illness became so serious that it did not seem humanly possible for me to recover.

I do not know how to describe that strange illness: I said things I did not think and did things as if I were forced to do them in spite of myself; I seemed to be delirious nearly all the time, but I am sure I never lost my reason for a moment. Sometimes I was in a coma for hours on end, unable to move at all; though all through it I was able to hear distinctly what anyone near me was saying, even in a whisper, and I can remember it to this day.

How the devil terrified me! I became frightened of everything. My bed seemed to be surrounded by frightful precipices; some nails in the wall of my room petrified me because they looked to me like great, black, charred fingers—until sometimes I had to cry out. One day, Father was looking down at me in silence, holding his hat, when suddenly it seemed to turn into a horrible shape. I showed such terror that poor Father went out sobbing.

But if God allowed the devil to attack openly, he also sent visible angels to console and strengthen me. Marie never left me nor gave any sign of being tired, in spite of all the trouble I must have been, for I could not bear to let her go away. When Victoire was looking after me at meal times, I never stopped crying and calling out: "Marie! Marie!" I only kept quiet when she wanted to go to Mass or to see Pauline. Léonie and my darling Céline did so much for me too. Every Sunday they used to spend hours shut up with a child who seemed to have lost her reason— O my Sisters, how you suffered for me!

Uncle and Aunt loved me very much too. My aunt came to see me every day and brought me lots of little delicacies. I can't say how much my affection for them grew through all this. Father had often said to us: "Remember, my dears, that your uncle and aunt are remarkably devoted to you." In his old age, he himself experienced their devotion, and now he must be watching over those who lavished so much love on him and repaying all their care.

Whenever the pain eased a little, I thoroughly enjoyed myself weaving crowns of daisies and forget-me-nots for the statue of Our Lady.

It was the lovely month of May, and the world was full of spring flowers; only the "little flower" was wilting. But there was a sun not far away to which the petals of the "little flower" would often turn—the statue of the Queen of Heaven. Father came into my room one morning on the verge of tears and went over to Marie. Sadly he gave her some gold coins and told her to have a Novena of Masses said at the shrine of Our Lady of Victories for the recovery of his "little queen." His faith and love touched me so much that I wanted to jump up and tell him I was cured, but this was not enough to work a miracle, and it needed a big one to bring me back to life—a very big one. But Our Lady of Victories obtained it!

It was one Sunday during the Novena; Marie went out into the garden, leaving me with Léonie, who was reading by the window. After a few minutes, I called out quietly, "Marie! Marie!" Léonie was accustomed to this sort of thing and took no notice, so I called louder, and Marie came back. I saw her quite clearly come in, and then for the first time I did not recognize her. Anxiously, I looked all around me, then toward the garden again, still calling, "Marie! Marie!"

I went through dreadful suffering during this struggle, yet Marie probably suffered even more. She went on trying to get me to recognize her, but without success, until finally she turned and whispered something to Léonie before she disappeared, pale and trembling.

At once Léonie carried me to the window overlooking the garden, and still without recognizing her, I saw Marie walking slowly up and down, holding out her arms to me, smiling and calling: "Thérèse! My darling Thérèse!" As even this failed, she came back in tears and knelt at the foot of my bed. Then, turning toward Our Lady's statue, she began praying for me with all the fervor of a mother interceding for her baby's life. Léonie and Céline began to pray too, and Heaven opened its gates in answer to their faith. As I could find no help on earth and was almost dying of misery, I, too, turned to my Heavenly Mother, asking her with all my heart to take pity on me now.

Suddenly the statue came to life, and Mary

appeared utterly lovely, with a divine beauty I could
not possibly describe. There was a wonderful sweetness and goodness about her face, and her expression
was infinitely tender, but what went right to my heart
was her smile. Then, all my pain was gone. Silently
two big tears trickled down my cheeks, tears of complete and heavenly happiness. Our Lady had come
to me! "How happy I am," I thought, "but I must
not tell anyone or this happiness will go away." When
I lowered my eyes, I recognized Marie at once. She
was looking lovingly at me and appeared to be very
moved, as though she half guessed what had just happened to me. I am quite sure I owed the wonderful
favor of Mary's smile to her prayers. Seeing my gaze
fixed on the statue, she said to herself, "Thérèse is
cured." And so she was. The light from her "gentle
sun" had revived the "little flower." Delivered once
and for all from her cruel enemy, she was alive again.
"*The dark winter was over and the rain was gone.*"
(Cf. *Cant.* 2:2). So well did Our Lady's "flower" flour-
ish, that four years later she was blooming in the fertile soil of Mount Carmel.

Marie, as I said, was sure that it was Mary who
had restored me to health and had half guessed the
rest as well. When we were alone, she pressed me so
delicately to tell her what it was that I could not
refuse, and I was so surprised to find how much she
had guessed—though I had said nothing—that I then
revealed everything. I had not been mistaken! At once
my happiness went, dissolved into bitterness, and for
four years the memory of that unforgettable favor
caused me nothing but pain. My happiness was

restored after that, and in all its fullness, at the Shrine of Our Lady of Victories as I knelt at her feet, and I will say more of that later.

But first, let me tell you my joy was turned to sadness. Marie listened to me as I told my story with childish simplicity and then asked me if she could tell them about it at Carmel, and I did not like to say no. It was such a joy to me on this visit to see you in your habit, and I think it was a wonderful moment for us both, with so much to talk about after all our suffering, though I could hardly say anything, I was so happy. I was treated very affectionately by Mother Marie de Gonzague, and I also saw several of the other nuns, all of whom asked me about my miraculous cure. Some wanted to know if Our Lady had been carrying the Child Jesus; others, if she had been accompanied by angels; and so on. All these questions worried me very much, and all I could say was: "Our Lady was very lovely, and I saw her come toward me and smile."

When I saw that they had such different ideas about it, I thought perhaps I had told them something wrong. If only I had kept my secret, I should have kept my happiness too! Our Lady was allowing me to go through all this for my own good. I should probably have become vain about it if it had been otherwise; as it was, all I got was humiliation and could only regard myself with contempt. Dear God, You alone know all that I endured!

Chapter 4

GROWING UP

IN writing about this visit to Carmel, my mind goes back to my first visit after you had entered. I had been wondering that morning what name they would give me when I got there; I could not bear to lose my lovely "Thérèse," yet I knew you already had a Thérèse of Jesus. I had a great devotion to the Child Jesus and suddenly thought how wonderful it would be if I could be called Thérèse of the Child Jesus. I never mentioned this to anyone, so you can guess how surprised and delighted I was when Reverend Mother said in the middle of our conversation: "When you join us, my Dear, you will be called Thérèse of the Child Jesus." This harmony of thought seemed a gracious sign from my beloved little Jesus Himself.

So far I have not said anything about how much I loved pictures and books, yet it is to the beautiful pictures you used to show me that I owe some of the greatest joys and the strongest inspiration in my efforts to practice virtue, and I lost all sense of time when I was looking at them. There was "The Little Flower of the Divine Prisoner," for example; I used to be quite carried away by all it suggested to me, and I told Jesus I would be His Little Flower; I wanted to give Him consolation, to draw near to the tabernacle, to be watched over, tended and gathered by Him.

As I was no good at games, I would have spent most of my time reading; luckily, I had visible guardian angels who guided me here and chose the sort of books I needed—books which nourished my mind and heart, as well as keeping me amused. I was only allowed a certain time for this favorite occupation, and it often meant great self-sacrifice, for I used to put my book away the moment time was up, even if I were halfway through a most fascinating passage. I must admit that, when I read certain tales of chivalry, I did not always grasp the realities of life; in my enthusiasm I wanted to do all the patriotic things the heroines of France had done, especially Joan of Arc.

It was at this time that I was given what I have always considered one of my life's greatest graces, for God did not enlighten me then in the way He does now. He taught me that the only glory which matters is the glory which lasts forever and that one does not have to perform shining deeds to win that, but to hide one's acts of virtue from others, and even from oneself, so that *the left hand does not know what the right hand is doing.* (Cf. *Matt.* 6:3). I was sure that I was born to be great and began to wonder how I should set about winning my glory; then it was revealed to me in my heart that my glory would lie in becoming a Saint, though this glory would be hidden on earth.

This aspiration may seem presumptuous, considering how imperfect I was and still am, even after so many years in religion; yet I am daringly confident that one day I shall become a great Saint. I am not relying on my own merits, because I haven't any. I hope in Him who is Virtue and Sanctity itself; He alone, content with my frail efforts, will lift me up to Himself, clothe me with His own merits and make me a Saint.

I did not realize in those days that one had to go through much suffering to become a Saint, but God soon brought this home to me by the trials I have told you about already.

But to go back to my story. Three months after I was cured, Father took me away for a delightful holiday, and I began to see something of the world. All around me was joy and happiness. I was entertained, pampered and admired; in fact, for a whole fortnight my path was strewn with flowers. But those words of the Book of Wisdom are only too true: "*The bewitching of vanity overturneth the innocent mind.*" (Cf. *Wis.* 4:12). When you are only ten, your heart is fascinated very easily, and I must admit that I found this kind of life charming. The world is able to combine so well the search for pleasure with the service of God, forgetting death, yet it has come to so many rich and happy young people I used to know. My mind goes back to their enchanting homes, and I can't help wondering what use to them now are those châteaux and estates where they enjoyed all the world could offer, and I realize that "*all is vanity save loving God and serving Him alone.*" (*Imit.* 1:1, 3).

I think Jesus wanted me to see something of the

world before He came to me for the first time, so that I might choose more surely that path on which I would promise to follow Him.

My First Communion will always be a perfect memory, and I am sure I could not have been better prepared than I was. Do you remember the wonderful little book you gave me three months before the great day? It was set out so beautifully and prepared me surely step by step; even though I had been thinking for so long about my First Communion, I had to renew my ardor and fill my heart with freshly gathered flowers. So every day, I made many sacrifices and acts of love, which were transformed into flowers; some were violets and roses, others cornflowers and daisies or forget-me-nots. I wanted all the flowers on earth to cradle Jesus in my heart. Marie took your place, and I spent hours every evening listening to all the lovely things she said to me. She passed her fine and generous spirit into mine, and as warriors of old used to teach their sons the use of arms, so she trained me for life's battle, stirring up my fervor by showing me the glorious palm of victory.

She told me, too, about the immortal riches one can amass so easily day by day, and of the foolishness of trampling underfoot the treasures one can make one's own by merely stooping to pick them up. She was so eloquent! I wished others could have heard her too, for in my simplicity I was sure she could have converted the most hardened sinners and made them leave the riches that will fade for those of Heaven.

I would have loved to be able to meditate, but Marie thought I was devout enough already and only let me say prayers. One of the mistresses at the Abbey asked me one day what I did with myself when I went home to Les Buissonnets. Shyly I told her: "Sometimes I go and hide myself in a little corner of my room which I can shut off with my bed curtains, and . . . just think." She laughed and asked: "But what do you think about?" "About God," I told her; "about how short life is, and about eternity . . . and . . . well . . . I just think." This little incident was not forgotten, and she often used to remind me of it and ask me if I still "thought." I realize now that I was really meditating, while the Divine Master was gently at work in my soul.

The three months of preparation for my First Communion passed quietly, and I soon found myself in retreat at the Abbey as a full boarder. It was a wonderful retreat. I do not think anyone can taste such happiness, except in a religious house. There were not many of us, so we could all have individual attention, and I could never express how grateful I was for the way our mistresses mothered us. I do not know why, but they seemed to watch over me more tenderly than over the others. The first mistress used to come every night with her little lamp and gently draw aside the curtains of my bed; then she would kiss me very tenderly on my forehead. She showed so much affection for me that one evening, touched by her tenderness, I said to her: "O Madame, I am so fond of you. I want to tell you a secret—a big secret." I had been hiding your precious little book from Carmel under my pillow, and now I drew this out to show her, my eyes shining. She opened it very carefully and then told me how lucky I was. Several times during my retreat I realized that there were very few motherless children who were looked after as tenderly as I was at that age.

I listened most attentively to Fr. Domin's conferences and took very careful notes, but I did not put down any of my own thoughts because I was sure that I should remember them quite easily, and so I did.

How delighted I was to be able to follow the Divine Office just like the nuns. You could have picked me out from the rest by the big crucifix Léonie had given me, which, like missionaries, I had fastened to my belt; and everyone thought I wanted to be like you. I thought of you so very often, for I knew that you too were in retreat; not, it is true, as I was, for Jesus to give Himself to you, but so that you could give yourself completely to Him, and on the very day of my First Communion. And so this quiet time of waiting was twice dear to me.

At last the most wonderful day of my life arrived, and I can remember every tiny detail of those heavenly hours: my joyous waking up at dawn, the tender, reverent kisses of the mistresses and older girls, the room where we dressed—filled with the white *snowflakes* in which one after another we were clothed—and above all, our entry into chapel and the singing of the morning hymn: "O Altar of God, Where the Angels are Hovering." I would not tell you everything, even if I could, for there are certain things which lose their fragrance in the open air, certain thoughts so intimate that they cannot be trans-

lated into earthly language without losing at once
their deep and heavenly meaning. How lovely it was,
that first kiss of Jesus in my heart—it was truly a
kiss of love. I knew that I was loved and said, "I love
You, and I give myself to You forever." Jesus asked
for nothing, He claimed no sacrifice. Long before that,
He and little Thérèse had seen and understood one
another well, but on that day it was more than a
meeting—it was a complete fusion. We were no
longer two, for Thérèse had disappeared like a drop
of water lost in the mighty ocean. Jesus alone
remained—the Master and the King. Had she not
asked Him to take away her liberty, the liberty she
feared? She felt so weak and frail that she wanted to
unite herself forever to His Divine Strength. And her
joy became so vast, so deep, that now it overflowed.
Soon she was weeping, to the astonishment of her
companions, who said to one another later on: "Why
did she cry? Was there something on her conscience?
Perhaps it was because her mother was not there, or
the Carmelite sister she loves so much." It was beyond
them that all the joy of Heaven had entered one small,
exiled heart, and that it was too frail and weak to
bear it without tears. As if the absence of my mother
could make me unhappy on the day of my First Communion! As all Heaven entered my soul when I
received Jesus, my mother came to me as well. Nor
could I cry because you were not there, we were closer
than ever before. It was joy alone, deep ineffable joy
that filled my heart.

That afternoon I was chosen to read the "Act of
Consecration to Our Lady." I expect they chose me

because I had lost my earthly mother so young; anyway, I put my whole heart into it and begged Our Lady to guard me always. I felt sure she was looking down on her little flower with love and still smiling that lovely smile which had cured me and delivered me, and I knew all I owed her; for it was she herself, that morning of the 8th of May, who placed Jesus in my soul, *"the flower of the field and the lily of the valley."* (*Cant.* 2:1).

When evening came that lovely day, Father led his little queen by the hand to Carmel, and there I saw you made the bride of Christ. I saw your veil, all white like mine, and your crown of roses. There was no bitterness in all my joy, for I hoped to join you and wait for Heaven at your side.

I was very moved by the family feast prepared at Les Buissonnets and delighted with the little watch which Father gave me, yet my happiness was very tranquil, with an inward peace no earthly things could touch. Night came at last to end my lovely evening, for darkness falls even on the brightest day. Only the first day of Communion in eternity will never end.

There seemed to be a veil of melancholy over the day that followed. My dresses, lovely as they were, and my presents—these could never fill my heart. Jesus alone could do that, and I longed for the wonderful moment when He would come a second time. This was on Ascension Day, when I had the joy of kneeling at the altar rails between Father and my darling Marie. Again there were tears of indescribable joy upon my cheeks, while I murmured time and time again the words of St. Paul: "*I live, now not I, but Christ liveth in me.*" (*Gal.* 2:20).

After this second visit of Our Lord, I longed for nothing but to receive Him. This was allowed on all the major feasts, but how far apart they seemed. Marie used to prepare me on the eve of these great days, just as she had done for my First Communion, and once I remember she spoke of suffering and said she was sure that God would always carry me like a little child and not make me tread that path. These words came back to me after Communion the next day, inflaming my soul with a desire for suffering, and I was convinced that there was many a cross in store for me. Then my soul was filled with such a flood of consolation as I have never had in all my life. Suffering began to attract me; I found charms in it which captivated me without yet fully understanding it. I felt another great desire: to love God only and find my joy in Him alone. Often during my thanksgivings, I repeated the passage from *The Imitation*: "O, Jesus! unspeakable sweetness, turn earthly consolations into bitterness for me." (*Imit.* III, xxvi, 3). These words came to my lips without any effort. I said them as a child recites what someone it loves has prompted, without fully grasping what it means. Later, I shall tell you, Mother, how Our Lord made this longing a reality, how He alone has been all my joy. But if I told you about that now, I would be anticipating, and I still have such a lot to tell you about my childhood days.

Soon after my First Communion, I went into retreat again for Confirmation, and I prepared myself with great care for the coming of the Holy Spirit; I can't understand how anyone could do otherwise before receiving this Sacrament of Love.

As it happened, the ceremony was put off, and I was only too glad to have a little longer in retreat. How happy I was! Like the Apostles, I waited for the promised Holy Spirit and was overjoyed that soon I would be a perfect Christian and have my forehead sealed eternally with the mystic cross of this great Sacrament.

There was no rushing wind, as on the first Pentecost, but just the gentle breeze which murmured on Mount Horeb to Elias. On that day I was given the strength to suffer, strength I was to need, for the martyrdom of my soul was going to begin very soon.

When this wonderful and unforgettable time came to an end, I had to return to my life as a day-boarder again. I got along well at lessons and quickly grasped the gist of things, but I found it very hard to learn by heart. All the same, I did very well in Catechism, and the Chaplain used to call me his "little doctor," probably because my name was Thérèse.

During playtime, I was quite happy to watch the games of the others from a distance, while I thought about serious things; that was what I liked doing most of all.

I used to amuse myself, too, with a game I made up; I would pick up the baby birds which had fallen out of the tall trees and give them an honorable burial in a little plot of ground which I turned into a cemetery.

At other times I used to tell stories, and even the

bigger girls came to listen; but as we were supposed to be exercising our bodies and not my tongue, it was just as well that our mistress forbade me to continue in my role of storyteller. I chose for my friends at that time two little girls about my age and learned from one of them how shallow mortal hearts can be. She had to go home to her family for several months. While she was away, I was very careful not to forget her, and I showed how pleased I was to see her again when she came back; but all I got from her was a look of indifference. She did not want me, and I felt it terribly. It was the last time I sought affection as fickle as hers, but God has given me such a faithful heart that once I love, I love for always, so I went on praying for her and love her even now.

Several of the others had a special affection for a certain mistress, and I wanted to copy them, but I found I couldn't. It was a happy failure and saved me a lot of pain. I thank Our Lord that He let me find nothing but bitterness in human affections. I should have been caught easily, and had my wings clipped, and then how could I have "*flown away and been at rest*"? (Cf. *Ps.* 54:7). How can a heart that is taken up with human love be fully united to God? I am sure it is not possible. I have seen so many people attracted by this false light, fly to it as moths do and burn their wings, then flutter, wounded, back to Jesus, the Eternal Fire which burns without consuming.

Our Lord knew that I was far too weak to face temptation; He knew that I would certainly have burned myself in the bewildering light of earthly things, and so He did not let it shine in my eyes. Where stronger souls find joy, but remain detached because they are faithful, I found only misery. I can't take any credit for not getting entangled in this way; it was only because God had mercy on me and preserved me. Without His help, I might have fallen even lower than St. Mary Magdalene. His wonderful words to Simon the Pharisee, "*to whom less is forgiven, he loveth less*" (*Luke* 7:47), echo so sweetly in my soul, for He has forgiven me much more than He forgave her. I can't really explain my feelings about this, but perhaps an example will give you an idea of what I mean: Suppose the son of a skillful doctor falls over a stone lying in his path and breaks a limb. His father hurries to help him and dresses his wound so skillfully that it heals completely. Naturally, he is quite right to love such a father and will be most grateful to him.

But supposing again this doctor saw the dangerous stone, anticipated that his son would fall over it and moved it out of the way when no one was looking; then his son would know nothing of the danger from which his father's loving care had saved him and so would have no reason to show gratitude. He would love him less than if he had healed some serious wound. But if he did find out the truth, surely his love would be even greater? I am that child, the object of the Father's loving providence, "*who did not send His son to call the just, but sinners.*" (*Luke* 5:32). He wants me to love Him because He has forgiven me, not *much*, but *everything*. He did not wait for me to love Him with a great love, like Magdalene's, but made me see that He had loved me first, with an infinite providence, so that now I may love Him in return even unto folly.

I have often heard it said in retreats and elsewhere that an innocent soul never loves God as much as a repentant one, and how I long to prove that that is not true.

Now I have wandered so far from my story that I do not know where to take it up again.

While I was making my retreat for my second Holy Communion, I was overcome by scruples. What a martyrdom! It lasted about two years, and no one could possibly understand what I had to go through, unless they had gone through it themselves. Every single thought and even my most commonplace actions became a source of worry and anxiety. I used to enjoy a momentary peace while I unburdened myself to Marie, but this used to cost me a lot because I thought I ought to tell her absolutely everything, even the wildest of my fancies. But this peace only lasted about as long as a flash of lightning, and I was back where I started. At least I made Marie practice wonderful patience!

During our holidays that year, we had a fortnight with our aunt at the seaside. She had always been wonderfully good to us—like another mother to the little girls from Les Buissonnets—and now she thought of everything to keep us amused: donkey rides and shrimping and so on. She used to spoil us, too, as far as our clothes were concerned. One day, I remember she gave me some sky-blue ribbon, and though I was twelve and a half, I was still childish enough to find extraordinary delight in tying my hair with it. But then I was overcome by so many scruples that I had to rush off to Trouville to Confession because I thought this childish pleasure must have been a sin.

I had one very useful experience while we were staying at Trouville. My cousin Marie was always having headaches. Her mother used to make a great fuss over her and call her all sorts of nice names, but Marie took no notice and just went on crying, "Oh, my poor head." I, too, used to have a headache, nearly every day, though I had kept it to myself, until one evening I thought I would follow Marie's example. I sat down in an armchair in a corner of the room and started crying. Soon my older cousin, Jeanne, whom I was very fond of, came and made a fuss over me, and then my aunt came in too and asked me what I was crying about. I said what Marie always said, "Oh, my poor head."

It seemed that complaining was not in my line, for no one would believe that I was crying because I had a headache. Aunt did not make a fuss over me as she usually did, but treated me as if I were a grown-up, while Jeanne reproached me in a pained tone of voice, though very gently, I must admit, because she thought I was guilty of lack of simplicity and confidence in my aunt by hiding the real reason for my tears, convinced that this was some dreadful scruple or other. In the end, I gave it up; it got me nowhere, and I made up my mind I would not try to imitate others again. That fable about the donkey and the dog was brought home to me; I was the donkey who had put his great hoof on the table because he wanted to be petted like the dog. And though I was not beaten like the poor donkey, I was certainly punished as I deserved and cured forever of my desire to attract attention.

The scruples I was telling you about ended by making me so ill that I had to leave school when I was thirteen. After that, Father sent me to a governess several times a week to finish my education. She was a very good teacher and I learned a lot from her, while at the same time I came into close contact with the world. I used to sit in her old-fashioned room with all my books and things around me while numerous visitors called. My governess' mother did most of the talking, but all the same I did not learn much, and though I used to keep my nose in my book, I heard all that went on and many things that it would have been better not to hear.

One lady said that my hair was very beautiful; another asked on her way out who the lovely young girl was. As I was not supposed to hear these remarks, they were all the more flattering, and the sense of pleasure they gave me shows only too well how vain I was.

I am sorry for people who lose their souls; it is so easy to miss your way when the paths of the world seem so attractive. Of course, enlightened souls find the pleasure which the world offers mixed with bitterness, while the immense void of their desires cannot be filled by a moment's flattery; but as I said before, if my heart had not been drawn toward God from its first awakening and if the world had smiled on me from the very moment I entered it, anything might have happened to me.

Dear Mother, with what gratitude I sing "*the mercies of the Lord*," for as the Book of Wisdom says, "*He has taken me away from the world, lest wicked men should alter my understanding, or deceit beguile my soul.*" (Cf. *Wis.* 4:11).

In the meantime, I made up my mind that I must consecrate myself in some special way to Our Lady, and so I joined the Children of Mary. I had to go to the convent twice a week then, and I must admit that this cost me a lot because I was still so shy.

I certainly loved our mistresses very much and will always be grateful for all they did, but as I said, unlike the other girls, I could never be friendly enough with any particular one to go and spend any length of time with her; so I used to work on in silence until the sewing class was over, and then, as nobody took much notice of me, I went into the tribune of the chapel until Father came for me. Here, in the silence, I found my one consolation: Jesus, my only friend. I could not open my heart to anyone else; conversations with other people—even about heavenly things—seemed tedious. It is true that my loneliness used to sadden me for a while, and I remember how often I would say that line from a beautiful poem that Father used to recite: "The world is but a ship, and not thy home"; young as I was, these words encouraged me, and although so many of my childish dreams have faded with the years, the symbol of a ship still charms me and makes my exile easier to bear. Does not the Book of Wisdom say: "*Life is like*

*a ship that passeth through the waves: when it is gone,
the trace thereof cannot be found.*" (*Wis.* 5:10).

When I think about these things, I seem to look
into infinity, to reach the eternal shore where Jesus
embraces me. I can see Mary coming to meet me with
Mother and Father and those four tiny angels, our
brothers and sisters. I already seem to enjoy that family life which lasts for all eternity. But before reaching
my heavenly home, I still had many more separations
to suffer on earth. The very year that I became a Child
of Mary saw me parted from my own Marie, my last
support, for after you had gone, it was she alone who
used to guide my soul, and I loved her so much that
I found life unbearable without her company.

As soon as I knew what she had decided to do, I
cried just as I did when you went and resolved that
I would take no more interest in anything on earth.

In any case, at that time I used to cry as much
over little things as big ones. For instance, I very
much wanted to practice virtue, but I went about it
in a very funny way. Céline used to do our room
because I had not learned how to look after myself
yet and did not do any housework—but occasionally
I used to make the bed or go to fetch Céline's little
plants and cuttings from the garden if she was out,
just to please God. As I said, it was "for God alone"
I did these things, so I should not have expected any
other reward; but I did, and if Céline did not seem
surprised or thank me for what I had done, I was
far from pleased about it and showed it by crying.
If ever I hurt anyone's feelings by accident, instead
of making the best of it, I was so disconsolate that

I made myself ill, and that made things worse. Then, if I got over the first mistake, I would begin to cry because I had cried. I seemed to make troubles out of everything then. Now things are quite different; God has given me the grace not to be disheartened by any transitory things, and when I look back on those days, my soul overflows with gratitude, for the graces I received from Heaven have so changed me that I do not seem to be the same person at all.

When Marie entered Carmel and I could not tell her about my scruples any more, I turned my attention to Heaven and had recourse to those four little angels who had gone on ahead. They never had had to bear scruples, so I thought they would be sure to take pity on their poor sister, still suffering on the way. I used to talk to them with all the simplicity of a child, reminding them that I was the baby of the family, the one upon whom our parents and sisters had showered most love and tenderness and that they would surely have done the same if they had stayed on earth. I could not see why they should forget all about me just because they had gone to Heaven. On the contrary, they could delve into divine treasures and could easily prove that one could still love up there by getting me some peace. I did not have long to wait for their answer! Peace soon filled my soul, and I knew that I was loved, not only by those on earth, but by those in Heaven too.

From that moment, my love for my little brothers and sisters in Heaven grew deeper. I loved to talk to them about the miseries of exile and tell them how much I longed to join them in our eternal home.

Chapter 5

CHRISTMAS GRACE AND AFTER

I CERTAINLY did not deserve all the graces Our Lord gave me, for though I really did want to be good, I was full of imperfections. I made myself almost unbearable by being far too sensitive, and nothing that was said to me seemed to help me overcome this tiresome fault.

I do not know how I could think of entering Carmel when it needed a miracle to overcome my childishness, but as it happened, God did work this miracle on Christmas Day in 1886; the Divine Child, scarcely an hour old, flooded the darkness of my soul with radiant light.

By becoming little and weak for love of me, He made me strong and full of courage, and with the arms He gave me, I went from one victory to another, and began to "*run as a giant.*" (*Ps.* 18:6).

My tears were dried up at their source, and after that, I hardly ever cried again.

I must tell you how the precious grace of this complete conversion was granted me.

When I got home to Les Buissonnets from Midnight Mass, I knew that I should find my shoes standing at the fireplace, filled with presents, as I had always done since I was little, so you can see I was still treated as a baby.

Father used to love to see how happy I was and hear my cries of delight as I took each surprise packet from my magic shoes, and his pleasure made me happier still. But the time had come for Jesus to cure me of my childishness; even the innocent joys of childhood were to go. He allowed Father to feel cross this year, instead of spoiling me, and as I was going upstairs, I heard him saying: "Thérèse ought to have outgrown all this sort of thing, and I hope this will be the last time." This cut me to the quick, and Céline, who knew how very sensitive I was, whispered to me: "Don't come down again just yet; you'll only go and cry if you open your presents now in front of Father."

But I was not the same Thérèse any more; Jesus had changed me completely. I held back my tears, and trying to stop my heart from beating so fast, I ran down into the dining room. I picked up the shoes and unwrapped my presents joyfully, looking all the while as happy as a queen. Father did not look cross anymore now and entered into the fun of it, while Céline thought she must have been dreaming. But this was no dream. Thérèse had gotten back forever the strength of mind she had lost at four and a half.

That glorious night, the third period of my life began, the loveliest of all, and the one in which I received the most graces. In one moment, Jesus, content with good will on my part, accomplished what I had been trying to do for years.

I could have said what the Apostles said: "*Master, we have labored all night and have taken nothing*" (*Luke* 5:5), but Jesus was even more merciful to me than to them, for He took the net in His own hands, cast it into the water and pulled it out full of fishes, making me too a fisher of men. Charity took possession of my heart, making me forget myself, and I have been happy ever since.

As I closed my Missal after Mass one Sunday, a picture of the Crucifixion slipped out a little way, and I could just see one of the wounds in Our Lord's hands, with blood flowing from it. A strange new thrill passed over me. It pierced my heart with sorrow to see His Precious Blood falling, with no one bothering to catch it, and I made up my mind, there and then, to stay in spirit at the foot of the Cross, to gather up the dew of heavenly life and give it to others.

The cry of Jesus as He died, "I thirst," echoed every moment in my soul, inflaming my heart with a burning love. I longed to satisfy His thirst for souls; I was consumed myself with this same thirst, and yearned to save them from the everlasting fires of Hell, no matter what the cost. Then Jesus stirred up my love even more by letting me see how pleased He was with these longings of mine. I had been hearing people talk about a notorious criminal called Pranzini, who had been condemned to death for several brutal murders, and as he was unrepentant, it was thought he was going to lose his soul. I longed to save him from this final tragedy, but though I did use every spiritual means in my power, I knew that by myself there was nothing I could do to ransom him; and so I offered for him Our Lord's infinite merits and all the treasures of the Church. Needless to say, deep down in my heart I was sure that he would be reprieved, but I wanted some encouragement to go on in my search for souls, so I said very simply: "My God, I am sure You are going to forgive this wretched Pranzini, and I have so much confidence in Your mercy that I shall go on being sure, even though he does not go to Confession or show any sign at all of being sorry; but because he is my first sinner, please give me just *one sign* to let me know." He answered me to the letter. Father never used to let me read the papers, but I didn't think I was being disobedient when I rushed to *La Croix* the day after he was executed and turned to the bit about Pranzini. Guess what I found! I was so moved that tears came to my eyes and I had to rush out of the room. He had gone to the scaffold without Confession or absolution and was being led to the block by the executioner when he suddenly turned around. The priest had been holding out a crucifix to him, and as if moved by some inspiration, he had seized it and kissed the Sacred Wounds three times. This was my sign, and it touched me very much, since it had been the sight of the Blood flowing from one of these very Wounds that had given me my thirst for souls. I had wanted to give them His Precious Blood to drink to wash their sins away, and here was my "first-born" pressing his lips to His Wounds. What a wonderful answer! After this, my desire to save souls grew day by day. Our Lord seemed to be whispering to me,

"*Give Me to drink*" (*John* 4:7), as He did to the woman of Samaria; and so, hoping to quench His thirst, I poured out His Blood on souls and offered them to Him, refreshed with this dew of Calvary, exchanging love for love.

God had lifted me out of my narrow world in a very short time, and I had taken the first step, but the road ahead was long. However, freed from my scruples and over-sensitiveness, my soul grew. I had always loved everything noble and beautiful, and now I had a great thirst for knowledge; not satisfied with what my governess was teaching me, I began to study other subjects by myself and learned more in a few months than I had ever done at school, though this zeal was probably just "*vanity and vexation of spirit.*" (*Eccles.* 1:14). As I was so impetuous, this was a very dangerous moment in my life; but God had fulfilled in me that prophecy in Ezekiel: "*Behold thy time was the time of lovers: and I spread My garment over thee. And I swore to thee and I entered into a covenant with thee, saith the Lord God, and thou becamest Mine. And I washed thee with water, and I anointed thee with oil. I clothed thee with fine garments and put a chain about thy neck. Thou didst eat fine flour and honey and oil and wast made exceedingly beautiful and wast advanced to be a queen.*" (*Ezech.* 16:8, 9, 13).

This is just what Jesus has done for me, and I could apply every single word to myself; but as the favors I have already told you about are proof enough, I am only going to tell you about the abundant food our Master set before me.

My spiritual life up to now had been nourished by

the "fine flour" of *The Imitation* and it was the only book which did me any good, because I had not yet discovered the hidden treasures of the Gospels. Much to everybody's amusement, I always used to have it with me, and my aunt would often open it at random and make me say by heart the first chapter she came to.

At fourteen my thirst for knowledge had become so great that God thought it was time to season the "fine flour" with the honey and oil of Fr. Arminjon's conferences on *The End of this World and the Mysteries of the World to Come*. As I read, I experienced that joy which the world cannot give, something of what God has prepared for those who love Him. All our sacrifices seemed quite petty compared with this reward, and I wanted so much to love Jesus with my whole heart and prove it in a thousand ways while I still had the chance.

Since Christmas, I had taken Céline completely into my confidence, and Jesus, who wanted us to go forward side by side, bound our hearts together with ties far stronger than those of blood, and made us sisters in spirit too, so that the words of St. John of the Cross came true for us:

> Lightly the maidens tread the way
> Thy footsteps passed, Beloved One;
> The touch of the spark
> And the spicèd wine
> Bring to their lips the fragrant words
> Of love divine.

Our hearts were certainly light as we followed in

His footsteps; the sparks which He scattered in our souls, the spiced wine He offered us to drink made us oblivious of everything on earth, and aspirations full of love sprang to our lips.

I remember so well the times we spent together; when evening came, we used to sit at the attic window and gaze out into the deepening blue of the sky, scattered with golden stars, and as we gazed, I am sure grace was being poured into our souls; for God, as *The Imitation* says, "sometimes gives Himself to us in radiant light, sometimes veiled in symbols and in shadows." (Cf. *Imit.*, III, xliii, 4).

It was veiled in this way that He showed Himself to us, but the veil was so light that we could almost see through and there was no room for doubt. Faith and hope gave way to love; we had found already the One we were seeking, and *"when we were alone He gave us His kiss, and now no one may despise us."* (Cf. *Cant.* 8:1).

Such graces were not barren. The practice of virtue became attractive and seemed to come more naturally. At first, my face often betrayed my inward struggle, but little by little, sacrifice, even at the first moment, became easier.

Our Lord promised that *"to everyone that hath shall be given, and he shall abound"* (*Luke* 19:26), and every time I made good use of any grace, He gave me many more. He gave me Himself in Holy Communion far more often than I had dared to hope, for I had made it a rule that I would go only as often as my confessor permitted, without ever asking to go more frequently. I would act very differently now. I am convinced that one should tell one's spiritual director if one has a great desire for Communion, for Our Lord does not come from Heaven every day to stay in a golden ciborium; He comes to find another heaven, the heaven of our soul in which He loves to dwell. Jesus, who knew my longing, inspired my confessor to let me go to Holy Communion several times a week, and how delighted I was to be given this permission straight from Him.

I did not dare talk about my inmost feelings at that time. My way was so straight and obvious that I did not feel I needed any other guide but Jesus. I thought of spiritual directors as mirrors which faithfully reflect Our Lord for others, but in my case He did not have to use such a medium; He could act directly. Just as a gardener lavishes his care upon the fruit he wants to ripen early—not to see it hanging on the tree, but because he wants it to adorn his table for some feast—so Jesus lavished favors on His "little flower."

When on earth, He had exclaimed with joy: "*I bless Thee, O Father, because Thou hast hidden these things from the wise and the prudent, and hast revealed them to little ones.*" (*Luke* 10:21). Now He wished to manifest His mercy through me. Just because I was so little and so frail, He stooped to me and taught me gently the secrets of His love.

As St. John of the Cross says in his *Canticle of the Soul*:

> I had no guide, no light,
> Save that which burned within my heart,

And yet this light did guide my way,
More surely than the noonday sun
Unto the place where waited One
Who knew me well.

This place was Carmel, but before I could *"sit down under His shadow whom I desired"* (*Cant.* 2:3), I had to go through many tribulations. Yet the divine call was always so urgent that, even if it had meant going through fire, I would have cast myself in to follow Him.

I found only one soul to encourage me in my vocation, and that was you, my darling Pauline. My heart found in yours a faithful echo, and without your help, I should certainly never have made the harbor which you had reached five years before.

For five years I had been separated from you, and I had begun to think I had lost you, but in the hour of trial, it was your hand that showed me the road to follow.

I really needed this encouragement because visiting time had become almost unbearable; whenever I said anything about wanting to enter Carmel, I seemed to be discouraged. Marie thought I was too young and did all she could to stop me, and from the start, there seemed to be obstacles whichever way I turned. On top of that, I did not dare say anything to Céline about it, and it hurt me to keep silence, because I hated hiding anything from her. It was not long before she found out what I wanted to do, and far from trying to stop me, she accepted the sacrifice with wonderful courage. As she wanted to be a nun too, she ought to have gone first, but like the martyrs of old who used to say farewell with joy to those who were chosen to go into the arena first, she let me go and was as concerned about my difficulties as if it were her own vocation they affected. So I had nothing to fear from Céline, but I did not know how I was going to tell Father what I wanted to do, for how could I talk to him of giving up his "little queen" when he had sacrificed his two eldest daughters already? During that year, too, he had had a bad attack of paralysis, and though he had gotten over it quickly, it left us very worried about what the future might hold for him.

What a battle I had with myself before I could tell him, yet I had to make up my mind, for I was nearly fourteen and a half; and it was only six months to Christmas, the first anniversary of my conversion, and the day on which I had resolved to enter Carmel.

I chose the Feast of Pentecost to tell my secret. I prayed to the Holy Ghost all day for light and begged the Apostles to pray for me and inspire me with what to say, for surely they were just the ones to help a timid child destined by God to be, by means of prayer and sacrifice, an apostle of apostles.

It was in the evening, on coming home from Vespers, that I found my chance. Father was sitting out in the garden with his hands clasped as he drank in nature's loveliness. The setting sun's last rays were gilding the treetops where birds were singing their evening prayer.

There was a look of Heaven on Father's noble face,

and I felt sure his heart was filled with peace. I sat down beside him, not saying a word, but there were tears in my eyes. He looked at me more tenderly than I can express, pressed my head to his heart and said: "What is it, Little Queen? Tell me." Then, to hide what he was feeling too, he rose and walked slowly up and down, still holding me all the while close to his heart. Through my tears I told him about Carmel and my longing to enter soon, and then he too began to weep, but never said a word against my vocation, only that I was still rather young to make such a serious decision. When I insisted and gave him all my reasons, his upright, generous heart was soon convinced. We went on walking for a long time; my heart grew light again, and Father dried his tears, talking to me just like a Saint. Going to a low stone wall, he showed me some little white flowers, like very small lilies; then he picked one of them and gave it to me, explaining how carefully God had brought it to blossom and preserved it till that day. So striking was the resemblance between the little flower and little Thérèse that it seemed as if I were listening to the story of my own life. I took the flower as if it were some relic, noticing that when Father had tried to pluck it, the roots had come out too, but quite undamaged, as though destined to start life again in some other and more fertile soil. Father was doing just the same for me, by letting me be transplanted to Mount Carmel from the lovely valley which had been the scene of my life's first steps.

I fastened the little flower onto a picture of Our Lady of Victories; the Child Jesus seemed to hold it in His hand, and so it has remained, except that now the stalk is broken near the root.

I am sure that this is God's way of telling me that it will not be long before He severs the roots of His little flower, and that she will not be left on earth to fade.

Father had given his consent, and so I thought I could fly to Carmel with no more ado, but as soon as I told Uncle my secret, he said it appeared to him against all human prudence for me to enter such a strict Order when I was only fifteen and that it would do religion great harm if a child were allowed to embark on a life like this. He finished by saying that, as far as he was concerned, he was completely against it and only a miracle would make him change his mind. I saw that it was useless to argue and left with my heart full of misery.

Prayer was my one consolation. I asked Jesus to work the miracle necessary before I could respond to His call. Time passed, and my uncle seemed to have forgotten all about our interview, though I found out later that actually it had been constantly on his mind.

Before allowing a single ray of hope to shine upon my soul, Our Lord made me endure another kind of martyrdom, which lasted three days, and it was not until then that I understood what Our Lady and St. Joseph suffered as they searched the streets of Jerusalem for the Child Jesus. I seemed to be lost in some frightful desert, or like a little boat without a pilot, at the mercy of the storm-tossed waves. I knew that Jesus was there, asleep in my barque, but the night was so dark that I could not see Him. If only the storm had broken, a flash of lightning might have pierced through the clouds; it would not have been much, but at least I should for a moment have seen my Beloved. But there was only night, dark night, utter desolation, like death itself.

Like Our Lord in the agony in the Garden, I felt forsaken and could find no consolation, either on earth or in Heaven. Nature seemed to share my bitter sadness; the sun did not shine once during those three days, and it rained hard all the time. And this is not the only time nature has reflected the feelings in my heart; I have noticed it often during my life. When I cried, the heavens were full of tears, and when I was happy, the sky was a cloudless blue.

On the fourth day—it was a Saturday, I remember—I went to see my uncle again, and to my great surprise, I found that his attitude toward me had completely changed. Without waiting for me to say why I had come, he took me into his study, and then after reproaching me gently for being rather reserved with him, he told me that he did not need a miracle anymore; he had asked God to enlighten him, and his prayer had been answered. I hardly knew him. Like a loving father, he took me in his arms as he finished, saying: "Go in peace, my dear. You are a little flower whom Our Lord has chosen and wants to gather for Himself. I won't stand in the way." My heart was singing as I returned to Les Buissonnets; the clouds had all gone and the sky was a lovely blue, while the dark night in my soul had passed. Jesus had awakened and was filling me with joy, and the waves were silent. Instead of the howling wind, a gentle breeze was swelling my sails, and I thought I had already reached harbor. But there were storms ahead, storms that would make me fear at times that I was being driven away beyond return from the shore I longed so much to reach.

No sooner had I obtained my uncle's consent than you told me that the Superior of Carmel would not let me enter until I was twenty-one. The possibility of such serious opposition had not occurred to anyone, and it would be very hard to overcome; but I kept up my courage and went with Father to ask him if I could enter. He treated me coldly, and nothing would change his mind; we left in the end with a most emphatic "No," except that he added: "I am only the Bishop's delegate, of course, and if he allowed you to enter, I could not prevent it."

As we came out of the presbytery, we found that *it was pouring with rain again*, just as heavy clouds were once more darkening my soul. Father did not know what to do to comfort me, but promised to take me to Bayeux if I wanted, and I gratefully accepted.

Many things, however, happened before this trip was possible, and in the meantime, my life, to all outward appearances, went on as usual. I continued my studies, but most important of all, I went on growing in the love of God, so much that sometimes my soul experienced real transports of love.

One evening, not knowing how to tell Jesus how much I loved Him and how I wanted above all else to serve Him and give Him glory, I was saddened at the thought that He would never receive a single act of love from the depths of Hell. Then, from the bottom of my heart, I said I would consent to be cast into that place of torment and blasphemy, so that even there He would be loved eternally. This could not glorify Him, of course, because it is only our happiness He desires, but when one is in love, one says so many foolish things. Even while I spoke like this, I still had an ardent desire for Heaven, though Heaven meant nothing to me, save love, and I was sure that nothing could take me from the Divine Being who held me captive.

It was at this time that Our Lord gave me the consolation of a deeper understanding of a child's soul, and this is how it came about.

A poor woman had been taken ill, and I was giving a good deal of my time to looking after her two little girls, both under six. It was a real joy to see the way they believed everything I told them. Baptism does indeed plant the seeds of the theological virtues deep in our soul, for the hope of the joys of Heaven, even from our earliest days, is quite strong enough to encourage the practice of self-sacrifice.

I did not speak of toys or sweets when I wanted these little girls to be kind to each other, but of the eternal reward the Child Jesus would give to good children.

The elder one, who had just reached the use of reason, used to look very happy about it and ask a host of delightful questions concerning little Jesus and His beautiful Heaven. She promised faithfully that she would always give way to her sister and said she would never forget what the "tall young lady," as she used to call me, had told her. Innocent souls like these, I thought, were like soft wax, ready for any impression, evil ones, unfortunately, as well as good. I understood what Jesus meant when He said: "*It were better to be thrown into the sea than to scandalize one of these little ones.*" (*Matt.* 18:6).

How many souls might reach a high degree of sanctity if properly directed from the first. I know God can sanctify souls without help, but just as He gives the gardener the skill to tend rare and delicate plants while fertilizing them Himself, so He wishes to use others in His cultivation of souls. What would happen if the gardener were so clumsy that he could not graft his trees properly, or knew so little about them that he wanted to make a peach tree bear roses?

This reminds me that among my birds I had a canary which used to sing exquisitely, and a young linnet of which I took very special care, having adopted it from its nest. Poor little captive, deprived of its parents' singing lessons and hearing only the joyful trilling of the canary from morning to night, it tried one day to follow his example—no easy thing for a linnet to do! It was delightful to watch the efforts of the poor thing, whose soft voice was not made for the vibrant notes of its master, though much to my surprise, it did succeed and began to sing exactly like the canary. You know who taught me to sing when I was young—Mother—and whose voice enchanted me. Frail as I am now, I hope one day to sing eternally the "Canticle of Love," whose melodies I hear so often on earth.

But where am I? These thoughts have carried me

away, and I must go on with the story of my vocation.

On October 31, 1877, Father and I set off for Bayeux. My heart was full of hope, but I was still apprehensive at the thought of presenting myself at the Bishop's house; it would be the first time I had made a call without any of my sisters with me, and it was to be on a Bishop!

Until now, I had never had to do more than answer questions others put to me, and now I should have to explain why I wanted to enter Carmel and prove that my vocation was genuine.

It cost me a great deal to overcome my nervousness, but how true it is that nothing is impossible to love, since it is convinced "it may and can do all things." (*Imit.*, III, V, 4). Love of Jesus, and that alone, gave me the strength to face these difficulties and those which followed, the tribulations which were the price I had to pay for my happiness. I look upon them now as a very small price, and if I were to begin again, I should be prepared to pay a thousand times more.

Heaven seemed to have opened its floodgates as we entered the Bishop's house. The date of our visit had been fixed by the Vicar General, Fr. Révérony. He treated us with great kindness, although he seemed somewhat surprised.

There were tears in my eyes, and when he saw them, he said: "Diamonds! We mustn't make a display before His Grace!" The rooms we had to go through seemed so big that they made me feel like a little ant, and I wondered if I should have the

courage even to open my mouth. The Bishop happened to be with two priests, walking up and down
a corridor, and I saw the Vicar General go and speak
to him. Then they all came back together to the room
where we were waiting.

There were three vast armchairs standing before
the hearth, where a bright fire was burning. As soon
as the Bishop entered, Father knelt beside me for his
blessing, and then we were asked to sit down, Fr.
Révérony directing me to the chair in the middle.
When I politely excused myself, he insisted, telling
me to show that I could obey.

I did what I was told at once, without another
word, and was mortified by seeing him take an ordinary chair, while mine was so vast that it would have
held four of my size with ease—far greater ease than
I felt at the time.

I had been hoping that Father would do the talking, but instead of this, he told me to explain why
we had come. I did this as eloquently as I could,
knowing all the time that a single word from the
Superior would have done far more than anything I
could ever say, and the fact that he was opposed hardly
counted in my favor. The Bishop asked me if I had
been wanting to enter Carmel for a long time. "Yes,
my Lord," I answered, "for a very long time." Father
Révérony laughed and said: "Come now, it can't have
been fifteen years!" "That is true," I replied, "but it
has not been much less; I have wanted to give myself
to God since I was three."

His Lordship then tried to make me understand
that I should stay with Father a little longer, think-

ing that this would please him, and was surprised
and edified to find him on my side and saying with
all deference that we would be going on the dioce-
san pilgrimage to Rome and that I would not hesitate to speak to the Holy Father if permission were
not granted before then.

It was finally decided, however, that His Grace
would have to interview the Superior before coming
to any decision. Nothing could have depressed me
more, because I knew how determined his opposition was.

In spite of what Father Révérony had said, I not
only made a display of my diamonds before the
Bishop—I showered them on him!

He seemed very touched and treated me with far
greater tenderness, it appears, than he had ever shown
to any other child. "All is not lost, my daughter," he
said, "but I am very pleased that you are going with
your father to Rome; it will confirm you in your
vocation. You ought to be rejoicing, not crying. I am
going to Lisieux next week, and I will talk to the
Superior about what you want to do and will send
my answer to you in Italy."

Finally we were taken into the garden, and the
Bishop was highly amused when Father told him that
I had put my hair up only that morning, just to make
myself look a little older. He has never forgotten this,
as I know for a fact that he never speaks to anyone
about his "little daughter" without telling them this
story about her hair, while I heartily wish that nothing had been said about it.

The Vicar General took us to the door, remarking

that such a thing had never been seen before—a father just as anxious to give his child to God as that child was to offer herself.

So we were obliged to return to Lisieux without the desired answer. My future seemed shattered forever, and I seemed to be held up by more and more difficulties as I came closer to my goal; yet in the depths of my soul I never ceased to have the profoundest peace because I sought the will of God alone.

Chapter 6

TRIP TO ROME

THREE days after our pilgrimage to Bayeux, I set out on a far longer one, this time to the Eternal City. I saw splendid monuments, studied treasures of art and religion and, most wonderful of all, stood on the very soil that the Apostles trod, the soil bedewed with martyrs' blood; and from its contact with these sacred things, my soul grew strong, while I learned the emptiness of things that pass.

I am glad I went to Rome; only I can see why some thought Father took me on this pilgrimage to change my views about the religious life; a vocation not so secure might have been shaken. To start with, Céline and I found ourselves mixing with members of the aristocracy; in fact the pilgrimage seemed to be made up of them, but we were not impressed, and looked upon their high-sounding titles as nothing more than the "*vapour of smoke.*" (*Joel* 2:30). The words of *The Imitation*, "Do not be solicitous for the shadow of a great name" (*Imit.*, III, xxiv, 2), were not lost on me, and I realized that real nobility is in the soul, not in a name.

Isaias says that "*the Lord shall call His servant by*

another name" (Is. 65:15), and in St. John we read, "*To him that overcometh I will give a white counter, and on the counter a new name written which no man knoweth but he that receiveth it.*" (*Apoc.* 2:17).

We shall be told our titles of nobility in Heaven; "*then shall every man have praise from God*" (*1 Cor.* 4:5), and the one who chose for love of God to be the poorest and most obscure on earth will be the first and the richest and most glorious in Heaven.

This was one thing I learned; another was about priests. Up to then, the principal aim of the Carmelite Reform was a mystery to me; I was quite happy to pray for sinners, but the idea of praying for priests seemed surprising because I thought their souls must be crystal pure. But I grasped my vocation while I was in Italy, and this alone would have made the journey worthwhile. I met many saintly priests that month, but I also found out that in spite of being above angels by their supreme dignity, they were nonetheless men and still subject to human weakness. If holy priests, "the salt of the earth," as Jesus calls them in the Gospel, have to be prayed for, what about the lukewarm? Again, as Jesus says: "*If the salt shall lose its savour, wherewith shall it be salted?*" (*Matt.* 5:13).

What a magnificent vocation we have. It is for us in Carmel to preserve the "salt of the earth"; to be the apostles of the Apostles of Our Lord by our prayers and sacrifices, while they preach the Gospel to others by word and example. What a noble task! But I must not run on here, or my pen would never stop.

To go back to the journey itself, let me tell you

more details. Lisieux was still shrouded in darkness as we passed through its silent streets on the morning of November 4. I seemed to be off into the unknown with wonderful things in store for me. When we got to Paris, Father made us see all the sights, but for me, Our Lady of Victories was everything. I can't describe what I experienced at her Shrine. The graces she gave me there were like those of my First Communion, filling me with peace and happiness. In this sanctuary, Mary my Mother made it quite clear to me that it really was she who had smiled on me and cured me. With all my heart I begged her to keep me far from all occasion of sin and to make my dream come true by casting about me her mantle of virginity. I knew quite well that during this pilgrimage I should meet with things which might upset me. I knew nothing about evil and was afraid of finding it. "*To the pure all things are pure.*" (Titus 1:15). The simple and upright see no evil because it does not exist in inanimate things, only in impure hearts, but I had not found that out yet.

As devotion to St. Joseph had always from the beginning been closely bound up with my devotion to Our lady, I prayed to him that he might take care of me too, and I used to say every day the prayer, "St. Joseph, Father and Protector of Virgins." Under such patronage, I knew I was out of harm's reach.

We left Paris on November 7, after consecrating ourselves to the Sacred Heart in the Basilica of Montmartre. On the train, every compartment was given a Saint's name, the Patron Saint of a priest in the compartment or of his parish being chosen in his honor. In front of everybody, ours was named after St. Martin, and the compliment so moved Father that he went at once to thank Mgr. Legoux, the Vicar General of Coutances, who was directing the pilgrimage. After this, several people always referred to Father as "Monsieur St. Martin."

Father Révérony was keeping a sharp eye on me, and I could see this even at a distance; if I did not happen to be sitting opposite him at table, he used to lean forward so that he could see and hear what I was doing. He must have been satisfied, as he seemed in the end to be more favorable toward me; I say, "in the end," because as you will soon see, in Rome he was anything but my advocate!

Before reaching the goal of our pilgrimage, we had to go through Switzerland, with its towering mountains, whose snow-capped peaks were lost in the clouds, with its waterfalls and its deep valleys, rich with giant ferns and purple heather. This profusion of nature's loveliness did so much good to my soul, raising it to the God who had poured such wonders on a land of exile destined to endure for but a day. At one moment we were high upon the mountainside, with yawning chasms at our feet, ready to engulf us; at another, passing through a charming village with flimsy clouds lazily wandering over its chalets and graceful spire; then by a broad lake with calm, clear waters mingling their azure with the crimson of a setting sun. I cannot say what an impression the magnificence and grandeur of these scenes made upon me; it was a foretaste of Heaven's wonders. Then I thought of the religious life as it really is, with its restrictions and its little hidden sacrifices every day, and I saw how easily one might become so taken up with oneself that one might forget the glorious purpose of one's vocation. I thought to myself: "Later on, in the hour of trial, when enclosed in Carmel, I shall only be able to see a little corner of the sky; I will look back on today and be encouraged: the thought of God's majesty and greatness will put my own small troubles in their place. I will love Him alone and not make myself unhappy by being taken up with trivialities, now that I have caught a glimpse of what He has reserved for those He loves."

I turned my attention then from the works of God to those of men; Milan was the first Italian city we came to, and we were particularly interested in the white marble Cathedral there, which contained enough statues to populate a town. Céline and I left the more timid ladies of the party, who gave up after climbing the first flight of the tower steps, and followed the bolder pilgrims to the topmost turret, enchanted at the sight of the whole of Milan at our feet with its inhabitants like tiny ants. We came down from our vantage point and then set out on interminable carriage drives, which were to go on for a month and cure me forever of all desire for easy travelling. We were enthralled by the Campo Santo. The white marble statues in this vast cemetery were chiseled with such genius that they seemed alive, and all the more enchanting because seemingly placed at random. There was such a calm Christian sorrow on the faces of these works of art that one felt like consoling them. Here a child casts flowers upon its father's grave, and one forgets that the frail petals are of marble, as its fingers seem to let them fall; there a widow's fragile veil, or the ribbons in a maiden's hair, appear to tremble in the movement of the breeze. Seeing us speechless with admiration, and probably vexed because he could not feel as we did, an old gentleman who had been following us wherever we went said, "What enthusiasts these French are," though he was as French as we were. Poor man! He would have been better at home, as far as I could see; far from enjoying the journey, he was always grumbling, dissatisfied with the towns, the hotels, the people and everything else. Father, who was happy wherever he was, tried to cheer him up; he offered him his seat in the carriage and on other occasions too, and in his usual kind way, tried to get him to look on the bright side, but he was still miserable. How many different sorts of people we met, and how interesting the study of the world becomes when one is just about to leave it!

Venice brought a complete change of scene. No more the noise of the big town, but stillness, broken only by the soft lapping of the waters and the splashing of oars. It is an attractive yet melancholy city, and this melancholy envelops even the palace of the Doges for all its splendor. We passed through rooms whose vaulted roofs have long ceased to echo with the voice of Governors pronouncing sentence of life or death; prisoners are no longer buried alive in the gloomy dungeons, but the sight of those wretched cells made me think of the days of the martyrs, and

I would gladly have been imprisoned in that darkness for my faith.

I was awakened from my dreaming by the voice of the guide, and I crossed the Bridge of Sighs, so called because the prisoners, preferring death to the horrors underground, sighed with relief as they crossed it on the way to die.

After Venice, Padua, where we venerated the relic of St. Anthony; then Bologna, where St. Catherine's body lies; her face still bears the impress of the Infant Jesus' kiss. On to Loreto with my heart full of joy; Our Lady certainly chose an ideal setting for the Holy House, everything poor and simple and primitive, the women still in their charming national costumes, not as elsewhere in the latest Paris fashions, and I was enchanted.

But what of the Holy House itself? This very roof had once sheltered the Holy Family; Our Lord's divine eyes had gazed upon these walls; the earth had known the sweat of Joseph's toil, and Mary had here borne Jesus in her womb, then in her arms; how deeply I was moved! I saw the little room where the Annunciation took place and put my Rosary in the bowl once used by Jesus as a child. What enchanting memories these are!

The greatest joy of all was to receive Jesus in His own house and become His living temple in the very place where He had dwelt on earth. According to the Roman custom, the Blessed Eucharist is only reserved at one altar in each church, and the priest only gives Communion to the faithful from there; in Loreto this Altar is in the Basilica which enshrines the Holy

House like a priceless diamond in a casket of white marble. This would not do for us; it was in the *diamond*, not merely in its casket, that we wished to be given the Bread of Angels.

Father, docile as ever, followed the rest, but his daughters, who were more independent, made for the Santa Casa itself. A priest with special dispensation was saying Mass there, and we told him what we wished so much to do. This considerate priest at once asked for two small hosts and placed them on the paten. You can guess what a joy that Communion was, a joy beyond words. So what will an eternal Communion be like in the House of the King of Heaven? The joy of that will never be clouded by the sadness of farewell; there will be no need to steal fragments from the walls which His presence sanctified, for His house will be all our own forever and ever.

It is not His earthly house He wants to give us. He shows us that only to make poverty and the hidden life dear to us. It is His palace of glory that He is keeping for us, and we shall see Him then, not in the guise of a child or under the form of bread, but as He is, radiant in His infinite beauty.

I will tell you about Rome now, Rome where I looked for consolation and found the Cross. We arrived during the night. I had been sleeping in the carriage and was awakened by the shouting of porters: "*Roma! Roma!*"—a cry soon picked up and echoed enthusiastically by the pilgrims. It was no dream; I was in Rome. We spent our first and perhaps most enjoyable day outside the walls, where everything still retains its air of antiquity, while in the center of Rome the hotels and shops take one back to Paris. Our drive through the Roman campagna made a very deep impression on me, while I cannot say how thrilled I was in the Colosseum. Here at last I was seeing with my own eyes the arena where so many Martyrs had shed their blood for Jesus, and I wanted to stoop and kiss the soil which their glorious trials had sanctified. What a disappointment! The ground had been raised and the real arena was buried about twenty-six feet down. Out in the middle there was nothing but a mass of rubble where excavations had been going on, and even this was shut off by an insurmountable barrier. No one dared go in among such dangerous ruins. Yet could one possibly be in Rome and not go down? It was impossible, and from then on I did not take any notice of what the guide was saying: I could think of one thing only—I had to get down into the Arena. The Gospel tells us that Magdalene stayed close to the tomb, constantly stooping to look inside, and at last saw two angels. Constantly stooping as she did, I saw at last, not two angels, but at least what I was looking for, and with a cry of joy I said to Céline: "Follow me, there is a way through." We both ran forward at once, scrambling over the ruins, which crumbled under our feet, while Father shouted after us, astonished at our recklessness. But we did not hear. As warriors of old felt their courage grow in the face of danger, so our joy increased with our tiredness and the danger we faced to get to our longed-for goal. Céline, who was more far-sighted than I, had been listening to the guide, who was describing a small stone cross which marked the place where the martyrs had fought the good fight. So she began looking round for it, and it was not long before we were kneeling on the sacred spot, our hearts united in the selfsame prayer. My heart beat violently as I pressed my lips to the dust once reddened with the blood of the early Christians, and I asked the grace to be a martyr too for Jesus. At the bottom of my heart I felt that I was heard.

All this took only a short time, and having collected some stones, we returned to the walls, and the perilous climb began again. Father had not the heart to be cross with us when he saw how happy we were, and I saw he was even rather proud of our courage.

After the Colosseum, we went to the Catacombs. Céline and I managed to lie down together in what had once been the tomb of St. Cecilia and to scoop up some of the earth which her sacred remains had sanctified. I had no particular devotion to her before the pilgrimage, but after I had visited the house where she was martyred and heard her called the "Queen of Harmony," because of the song she sang in her virginal heart to her Divine Spouse, it was more than devotion that I felt; it was the love of friendship, and she became my patroness and intimate confidante. What delighted me about her was the way she abandoned herself to God and her unbounded confidence, which enabled her to purify souls who had never desired anything but the joys of the world.

I likened her to the spouse in the *Canticles*, finding in her the "*choir in an armed camp*," for her life was simply a magnificent song amid the greatest of trials. This did not astonish me because "the Holy Gospels lay ever on her breast," while in her heart reposed the Spouse of Virgins.

We visited the Church of St. Agnes, and that delighted me too, and I met again one of the friends of my childhood. I tried to get a relic of hers for you, Mother, and was at first unlucky. But while men were refusing, God came to my help; a little piece of red marble fell from a mosaic which dated back to the time of the gentle Martyr and landed at my feet. What a gracious gesture! St. Agnes herself had given me a keepsake from her own house.

For six days we looked at all the principal wonders of Rome; on the seventh, I saw the greatest of them all—Leo XIII.

I had longed for that day, yet dreaded it too, for it was to decide my vocation, and I had heard nothing from the Bishop of Bayeux. The Holy Father's sanction was my only hope. But I would have to ask for it first, and this involved speaking to him in front of Cardinals, Archbishops and Bishops. I trembled at the very thought.

On Sunday morning, November 20, we entered the Holy Father's private chapel in the Vatican and attended his Mass at 8 o'clock. His fervor at the altar, worthy of the Vicar of Christ, showed him to be really the *Holy Father*. The Gospel of the day contained these encouraging words: "*Fear not, little flock, for it hath pleased the Father to give you a kingdom.*" (*Luke* 12:32). A lively confidence took possession of my heart, my fears vanished, and I was sure the Kingdom of Carmel would soon be mine. I was forgetting His other words: "*I dispose to you as my Father hath disposed to Me a kingdom.*" (Luke 22:29). In other words, "I have reserved for you the cross of trial, to make you worthy of My Kingdom." "*Ought not Christ to have suffered these things and so enter into His glory?*" (*Luke* 24:26). "*If you desire to sit on His right hand you must drink the chalice which He has drunk Himself.*" (Cf. *Matt.* 20:22).

There followed a Mass of Thanksgiving, then the audience began. Wearing a simple white cassock and a white cape, Leo XIII was sitting on a raised throne, surrounded by prelates and other dignitaries of the Church.

As was the custom, each pilgrim came forward in turn, knelt down and kissed the foot of the Supreme Pontiff and then his hand, before receiving his blessing. Two of the Noble Guard then touched him on the shoulder as a sign to rise and pass on, giving place to the next one. No one uttered a word. I had made up my mind to speak when Fr. Révérony, standing on the right of His Holiness, announced in a loud voice that he absolutely forbade anyone to speak to the Holy Father.

I turned a questioning gaze upon Céline, with my heart beating wildly. "Speak," she whispered. A moment later I was on my knees before him, and had kissed his slipper. He gave me his hand; then I raised my eyes, brimming with tears, to his and began my appeal: "Most Holy Father, I want to ask you a great favor." He bent his head at once, his face almost touching mine, while his piercing black eyes seemed to be gazing into my soul. I began again: "Most Holy Father, in honor of your Jubilee, let me enter Carmel at fifteen." The Vicar General of Bayeux was startled and far from pleased. "Your Holiness," he interrupted, "this is a child who wants to enter Carmel; the superiors are already going into the question."

"Very well, my child," said His Holiness, "do what the superiors decide." I clasped my hands and placed them on his knee while I made a final effort. "Holy Father, if you said yes, everyone else would be willing." He gazed at me steadily and said, stressing every syllable: "Well . . . Well . . . You will enter if it is God's will."

As I was about to say more, two of the Noble Guard signed to me to get up, and when they saw that that was not enough and that I stayed where I was with my clasped hands upon his knee, they pulled me up, with the help of Fr. Révérony. As they did so, the Holy Father gently touched my lips with his hand, then lifted it in blessing. His eyes followed me a long way.

Father had been in front of me and had no idea what had happened; he was most distressed to see me coming from the audience in tears. The Vicar General had been more than kind to him, presenting him as the "Father of two Carmelites," and Leo XIII had laid his hand on his head in sign of special favor, placing on him, as it were, a mysterious seal, in the very name of Christ.

Now that the "Father of *four* Carmelites" is in Heaven, there rests upon his forehead, not the touch of Jesus' representative, but the hand of the Spouse of Virgins, the King of Heaven. His divine Hand will rest forever on the brow which He has crowned with so much glory.

I was very much distressed, but since I had done everything I possibly could to respond to God's call, I must admit that, despite my tears, there was a great peace deep down in my heart, but only in the depths, for all the rest was bitterness. Jesus was silent—almost not there at all—for there was nothing to betray His presence.

The sun did not dare shine that day either. Dark clouds filled the lovely blue of the Italian sky, whose tears were mingling unceasingly with mine. It was all over; my journey was to no purpose, its enchantment at an end.

I ought to have been encouraged by the last words of the Holy Father, for they were really prophetic. In spite of all obstacles, God accomplished what He willed, bending the will of creatures to His own.

For some time now, I had been offering myself to the Child Jesus as His little plaything, telling Him not to treat me as the sort of expensive toy that children only look at, without daring to touch. I wanted Him to treat me like a little ball, so valueless that it can be thrown on the ground, kicked about, pierced and left lying in a corner, or pressed close to His heart if He wants. In other words, I wished only to amuse the Child Jesus and let Him do with me exactly as He liked. Jesus had heard me, and in Rome He pierced His little plaything, because He wanted, I expect, to see what was inside; then, satisfied with what He found, He dropped His little ball and fell asleep. What did He dream about? What happened to the abandoned little ball?

Jesus dreamed that He was still playing, that He kept picking up His little ball and throwing it down again, that He rolled it far from Him, but in the end, held it close to His heart, never to let it slip from His hands again. You can guess how sad the little ball was, left lying on the ground, though it went on hoping against hope.

Soon after the audience, Father had gone to see Brother Simeon, the Founder and Director of St. Joseph's College, and who should he meet there but Fr. Révérony. He reproached him gently for not helping me through my ordeal and told Brother Simeon all about it. The kind old man listened with great interest and even made notes about it, saying with feeling: "That sort of thing does not happen in Italy."

The day after the unforgettable audience, we had to leave for Naples and Pompeii. Vesuvius, with a dense column of smoke rising from its crater, fired a salute in our honor. While the havoc it had wrought in Pompeii was frightful, the power of God was there: "*He looketh upon the earth and maketh it tremble; He toucheth the mountains and they smoke.*" (*Ps.* 103:32). I longed to walk alone amid the ruins and ponder how transient all things human are, but such solitude was not to be thought of.

While in Naples, we went for a magnificent drive up to the Monastery of San Martino, high on the hill which overlooks the city. On the way back, our horses took the bit between their teeth, and I'm sure it was only because our Guardian Angels were looking after us that we arrived safe and sound at our splendid hotel. And it *was* a splendid hotel; we had been staying at the best hotels, like royalty, all the time. I had never been in such luxury. I should have been a thousand times happier under a thatched roof with a hope of entering Carmel than I was in the midst of gilded apartments, marble staircases and silk hangings, while my heart was in anguish. I learned from experience that joy does not reside in the things about us, but in the very depths of the soul, that one can have it in the gloom of a dungeon as well as in the palace of a king. I am happier now in Carmel amid exterior and interior trials than I ever was in the world, where I had all I wanted, and above all so happy a home.

Though my heart was plunged in sadness, I did not let it show outwardly because I thought I had kept my petition to the Holy Father a secret, but I soon found I was wrong. One day, when Céline and I were alone in the carriage, waiting for the others who had gone into a buffet, Mgr. Legoux appeared at the carriage door; he looked at me for some time, then said with a smile: "And how is our little Carmelite getting on?" I knew then that my secret was out, and various glances of sympathy in my direction only confirmed the fact, though luckily no one ever said anything to me about it.

Then there was my little adventure in Assisi. We had been visiting the places hallowed by St. Francis and St. Clare when I lost the buckle of my belt in the Monastery. It took me so long to find it and fix it on to the belt again that I was some distance behind the others, and by the time I had gotten to the door, there was only one carriage left. It belonged to the Vicar General of Bayeux. Should I run after the carriages already out of sight or ask Fr. Révérony for a seat in his? I did not want to risk losing the train, so I decided that the latter course was the wiser. I tried to look quite composed in spite of the fact that I felt most embarrassed, and I explained my dilemma. This put him in an embarrassing position too, because his carriage was already completely full, but one of the gentlemen got out at once and made me take his place, while he took a humble seat by the driver.

I felt like a squirrel in a cage, far from being at ease with important people all around me, and the most redoubtable and formidable of all directly opposite. As it turned out, he was very kind to me, and every now and then he would interrupt his conversation to talk to me about Carmel. He promised me that he would do everything he possibly could to realize my desire to enter at fifteen.

This promise was balm to my wounds, although it did not put an end to my suffering altogether. I had lost all confidence in mankind and was depending only on God, but my sadness did not prevent my taking a lively interest in the holy places we visited.

I was so glad to see the Shrine of St. Magdalene of Pazzi in the Choir of the Carmelite Church in Florence. All the pilgrims wanted to touch the Saint's tomb with their rosaries, but as I was the only one with a hand small enough to go between the bars of the grating, the honorable task fell to me. I was proud to do it, but it took a very long time.

This was not the first time I was so fortunate. Once when we were in Rome, venerating the relic of the True Cross at Santa Croce, with two of the Thorns and one of the sacred Nails, I lingered behind to have more time to examine them, and as the monk who was looking after them was taking them back to the altar, I asked him to let me touch them. He said I might, though he did not seem to think I would be able to. I slipped my little finger through an opening in the reliquary, and was able to touch the nail once covered with the Blood of Jesus. As you can see, I was treating Him as a child would who thinks it can do what it likes, looking upon its father's treasures as its own.

From Florence to Pisa, on to Genoa, and then began the return journey to France. The route by which we came back was really lovely, the railway running alongside the sea for miles, so close at one point that the stormy waves seemed almost on top of us—then through plains rich with orange groves, olives and slender palms. When evening came, the seaports were all ablaze with glittering lights, while up above, the first stars trembled in the darkening blue. My fairyland faded, leaving no regrets, for my heart was set on far more wonderful things.

Nevertheless, Father was already planning another journey, this time to Jerusalem; naturally, I should have liked to visit the places hallowed by the feet of Our Lord, but I was weary of earthly pilgrimages; longing only for the beauties of Heaven, I wanted to become a prisoner as soon as possible to win them for others.

Though I knew I still had to struggle and suffer before I saw the gates of my blessed prison open to let me in, I lost none of my confidence. I should enter on December 25, Christmas Day.

Home again in Lisieux, we went to Carmel. But what an interview! I expect you remember it, Mother. At the end of my resources, I left it all to you, and you said I should write and remind the Bishop of his promise. I lost no time in doing as you advised, and once the letter was in the post, I was sure he would say I could enter immediately.

Every day a fresh disappointment. Christmas came, with all its beauty, and Jesus slept on. He left His little ball upon the ground and never so much as looked at it.

What a trial! But He whose Heart is ever watchful taught me that He works miracles even for those whose faith is like a tiny mustard seed, to make it grow, while, as in the case of His Mother, He works miracles for His dearest friends only after He has tested their faith. He let Lazarus die, even though Martha and Mary had sent word that he was sick; and when He was asked by Our Lady at the marriage feast of Cana to help the master of the house, He said His time had not yet come. But after the trial, what rewards! Lazarus rises from the dead, and water becomes wine. This is how her Beloved dealt with His Thérèse—a long testing, and then He realized all her dreams.

January 1, 1888—My New Year's present from Jesus was the Cross. I had a letter from Mother Mary Gonzaga to say the Bishop's answer had come on December 28, authorizing my entry at once, but that she had decided to wait until after Lent. I burst into tears at the thought of such a delay. What a peculiar trial! The dove was free to fly to the ark, but the ark refused to let her in.

Those three months were rich in sufferings, but richer still in graces. At first I saw no reason why I should add to my sufferings any longer by such a strict life, but God made me realize the value of the extra time He gave me; I made up my mind to more serious mortification than ever. When I say mortification, I do not mean the sort of penance the Saints undertake. I was not like those grand souls who practice all kinds of penances from childhood. My mortification consisted in checking my self-will, keeping back an impatient word, doing little things for those around me without their knowing and countless things like that.

By these little things, I made ready to become the spouse of Jesus, and I cannot tell you how I grew in abandonment, humility and other virtues as a result.

Chapter 7

CARMEL

MONDAY, April 9, 1888, was chosen for my entry. It was the day you kept the Annunciation at Carmel, transferred because of Lent. The evening before, we all gathered around the family table, the last time for me, and it nearly broke my heart. Just when I would have liked to have had no notice taken of me at all, everyone spoke to me most tenderly! It made me feel the sacrifice of parting all the more.

The next morning, I had a last look around at Les Buissonnets, the charming cradle of my childhood— then I was off to Carmel.

I heard Mass, surrounded by those I loved, as I had been the evening before. At the Communion, when Jesus had come into our hearts, their sobbing was all I could hear; I did not cry at all myself, but as I headed the procession to the cloister door, my heart was thumping so hard that I wondered if I were going to die. It was a moment of agony which must be experienced to be understood.

I kissed the whole family, then knelt for Father's blessing. He knelt down too, and he was crying as he blessed me. It was a sight to gladden the Angels: an old man offering to God his child, still in the springtime of life. Then the doors of Carmel closed upon me. The two darling sisters who had each been a mother to me embraced me first, then my new Sisters, whose devotion and tenderness are beyond anything those in the world can guess.

My dream was at last realized, and peace flooded my soul, a deep, sweet, inexpressible peace, an inward peace which has been my lot these eight and a half years. It has never left me, not even when trials were at their height. Everything here delighted me, our little cell most of all; it was as though I had been transported to my far-away desert. But my happiness, I must say again, was a calm happiness.

Tranquil, unruffled by the slightest wind, were the waters on which the little boat was sailing under a sky of cloudless blue. All my trials had found an ample recompense, and profoundly happy, I kept saying over and over again: "I am here forever now." It was no mere transitory happiness, no passing illusion of one's first enthusiasm.

Illusions! Thanks be to God's mercy, I had none at all; the religious life was just what I had expected. No sacrifice took me by surprise, though as you know, Mother, the path on which I took my first steps was strewn with far more thorns than roses.

At first I found the daily bread of my soul dry and bitter; Our Lord allowed Reverend Mother to treat me with great severity, sometimes unconsciously. I could not meet her without getting some reproof or other. On one occasion, I remember, I had left a cobweb in the cloister. In front of everyone, she said: "The cloisters are obviously swept by a fifteen-year-old; it is a disgrace! Go and sweep that cobweb away, and in the future be more careful!"

Now and then I had to go and spend an hour with her for spiritual direction; most of it was spent in scolding me, but the worst of it was that I did not know how to correct my faults: my slowness, for example, or my lack of generosity in carrying out my duties.

One day it occurred to me that she would surely like to see me spending my free time on some work or other, time usually set aside for prayer; so, without raising my eyes, I carried on with my needle-work. But as I wanted to be faithful to Jesus and do it all for Him, I never told anyone.

During my postulancy, our Mistress used to send me out to weed the garden at half-past four every afternoon. It cost me a lot, all the more because I was almost sure to meet Mother Mary Gonzaga on the way. On one such occasion she remarked: "Really, this child does nothing at all. There must be something wrong with a novice that has to be sent for a walk every day."

She always treated me like this. How I thank God, my darling Mother, for such a virile and valuable training. What a priceless grace! I do not know what would have happened to me if I had become *the pet* of the Community, as those outside seemed to think! I would probably have thought of my Superiors merely as human beings, instead of seeing Our Lord in them, and the heart that had been so well guarded

in the world would have fallen prey to human attach-
ments in the cloister. Luckily I escaped such a fate.

I can honestly say that, from the moment I entered,
suffering opened her arms to me, not only in the
trials I have already told you about, but in others
keener still; and I embraced her lovingly.

I declared my reason for coming to Carmel during the solemn examination before Profession: *"I have
come to save souls and above all to pray for priests,"*
and when one wants to attain some end, one must
take the means. As Jesus had made me realize that
the Cross was the means by which He would give
me souls, the more often it came my way, the more
suffering attracted me. For five years I followed this
course, though I was the only one to know it, and
this practice was nothing else but the hidden flower
I wanted to offer to Jesus, the flower whose perfume
none would breathe this side of Heaven.

Even Fr. Pichon was surprised at what God had
worked in my soul within two months of entering
Carmel; in his view, I was following a tranquil path,
while my fervor was truly that of a child.

If I had not found it very difficult to open my
heart, my interview with the good Father would
have resulted in abundant consolation; however, this
is what he told me after I had made a General
Confession:

"In the presence of God, Our Lady, the Angels and
all the Saints, I declare that you have never committed a single mortal sin. Thank God for giving you
such a grace without any merit on your part."

Without any merit on my part! That was not difficult to believe. I knew how very weak I was and how imperfect. My heart overflowed with gratitude.

I had suffered a great deal from the fear that I had stained the purity of my baptismal robe, and it seemed to me that this assurance from a spiritual director "combining knowledge with virtue," as our Mother St. Teresa desired, came from God Himself. He went on to say: "My child, may Our Lord always be your Superior and Novice Master."

He has, in fact, been all this to me, and my Spiritual Director too, though I do not mean I never opened my heart to my Superiors. Far from concealing what was going on there, I have always tried to be an open book to them.

Our Mistress was a real Saint, a perfect example of an early Carmelite. As it was her task to teach me how to work, I spent all my time in her company. I cannot tell you how good she was to me, or how much I loved and respected her; but in spite of all this, my soul did not open out. I did not know how to explain what was going on inside me; words failed me, and spiritual direction became a torture and a martyrdom.

One of our older Mothers seemed to understand how I felt, for she said to me in recreation one day: "I don't suppose you ever have very much to tell your Superiors."

"What makes you think that, Mother?"

"Because you have an extremely simple soul; however, it will be even more simple when you become perfect. The closer we come to God, the more simple we become."

How right she was; it was because I was so simple that I found it so difficult to lay open my soul to anyone, but this did not make it any less of a martyrdom. Today, I can express myself without the slightest difficulty and without losing any of my simplicity.

Jesus, as I said, has been my Spiritual Director. No sooner had Fr. Pichon undertaken the care of my soul than his Superiors sent him off to Canada; reduced to receiving only one letter a year, the *little flower* which had been transplanted to the mountain of Carmel soon turned to the Director of directors, and she blossomed in the shadow of His Cross, having His tears and His Precious Blood for a refreshing dew and His adorable Face for the sun.

I had not realized till then the richness of the treasures hidden in His adorable Face, and it was you who taught me how to find them; you, the first to penetrate the mysteries of love hidden in our Beloved's Face, just as you were the first of us to enter Carmel; you revealed them to me now, and I understood— understood more than ever before that here was true glory! He whose *"Kingdom is not of this world"* (*John* 18:36) taught me that the only royalty that counts consists in "being willing to be ignored and despised" (Cf. *Imit.*, I, ii, 3) and "to find one's joy in self-contempt." (Cf. *Imit.*, III, xlix, 7).

If only my face, like the Face of Jesus, "could be hidden from everyone" (Cf. *Is.*, 53:3), that none on earth might take any notice of me! I longed to suffer and to be despised.

Because our Divine Master has always led me along such a path of mercy and has never made me want anything without giving it to me, I have always found His bitter chalice sweet.

Soon after the beautiful ceremony of Marie's Profession, at the end of May, in 1888, when Thérèse, the Benjamin, had the joy of crowning her eldest sister with roses on her mystical marriage day, a new trial fell upon the family.

Since his first attack of paralysis, we had noticed that Father used to get tired very easily, and I had often noticed during our journey to Rome that his face betrayed pain and exhaustion, though what had struck me most of all was the wonderful way he was advancing in holiness. He had completely mastered his natural impetuosity, and earthly things no longer seemed to concern him at all.

Let me give you an example of this, Mother. During our pilgrimage, the days and nights we spent in our compartment seemed very long to some of the travelers, and they used to make up card parties, which often ended in quite a storm. They asked us to play one day, but we excused ourselves on the plea that we did not know enough about it. The time did not seem at all long to us, as it did to them; it was all too short to enjoy the magnificent views which opened out before our eyes.

They were obviously annoyed at this, but Father very calmly defended us, leaving it to be understood that on a pilgrimage there ought to be a little more prayer! One of the players, forgetting the respect due to age, thoughtlessly remarked: "It's a good thing there aren't many more Pharisees about."

Father made no reply; he even seemed to take a

holy delight in the incident, and before long found an opportunity of shaking hands with the speaker, at the same time accompanying this fine gesture with so kindly a word that it appeared as if he had not noticed the other's rudeness, or at least had forgotten all about it.

But you know, Mother, that his habit of forgiving everyone began long before that. Mother and all who knew him vouched for the fact that he never spoke a single uncharitable word.

His faith and generosity were equal to every trial. This is how he told a friend of his about my leaving home: "Thérèse, my little queen, entered Carmel yesterday. Only God could ask such a sacrifice, but He helps me so much that my heart is filled with joy, even in the midst of tears."

Such a faithful servant deserved a fitting reward for his virtue, and you will remember, Mother, the reward he himself asked of God that day at visiting time when he said to us: "I have just returned from Alençon. In the Church of Notre Dame, I received such great graces and consolations that I prayed: 'It is too much, my God. I am too happy. This is not the way to Heaven; I want to suffer something for You, and I offer myself as a . . .'" The word "victim" died on his lips. He dared not say it in front of us—but we understood!

There is no need for me to remind you, Mother, of all our griefs; you know the heart-rending details well enough.

The time came for me to take the habit, and contrary to all expectations, Father had recovered from his second attack. The Bishop fixed the ceremony for January 10. I had had a long time to wait, but what a lovely day it was when it came. Nothing was lacking—not even *snow*. Have I ever told you, Mother, how fond I am of snow? When I was little, I used to be enchanted by its whiteness. I do not know how it began; perhaps it was because I was a little winter flower, and the first sight which met my baby eyes was the snow, like a lovely mantle, covering the earth.

Anyway, I wanted to see Nature clad like myself, in white, on my Clothing Day, but I had almost given up hope because it was so warm the day before that it might have been spring.

The 10th came, and the weather was just the same, so I gave up my childish desire as impossible of realization and went out to where Father was waiting for me at the cloister door. His eyes were full of tears as he came toward me. "Here is my little queen," he said, and pressed me to his heart, then he offered me his arm, and we made our solemn entry into the chapel.

It was his day of triumph, his last feast on earth. He had no more to offer; his whole family belonged to God, since Céline had told him that later on she too was going to leave the world for Carmel.

Overjoyed, he had replied in his incomparable way: "We must go at once to the Blessed Sacrament and thank Our Lord for the graces He has showered upon our family and for the honor He has done us in choosing His brides from my house, for it is indeed a great honor that He should ask me for my children. If I had anything better, I would not hesitate to offer it to Him."

"Anything better"—he had himself! *"And God received him as a victim of holocaust; He tried him as gold in the furnace, and found him worthy of Himself."* (*Wis.* 3:6).

The sacred ceremony over, as I was returning to the convent, the Bishop intoned the *Te Deum.* A priest told him that this hymn of thanksgiving should only be sung at a nun's Profession, but having been begun, it was sung right through. Perhaps it was only fitting that a feast day which summed up all the rest should be so crowned.

The moment I set foot in the cloister, my eyes fell upon my little statue of the Child Jesus smiling at me from the midst of flowers and lights. I turned towards the quadrangle and—*I saw that it was completely covered in snow!* What delicacy on the part of Jesus! To gratify His little bride's every desire, He had sent her snow! What mortal man could ever cause one flake to fall from the sky to charm the one he loves? Everyone was really astounded because the temperature was all against it, and I know that since then, many, on finding out that I had such a strange love of snow and about my wish, often call it "the little miracle" of my Clothing.

So much the better if it were a little strange; it only goes to show the unbelievable condescension of the Spouse of Virgins, who loves His lilies to be white as snow.

The Bishop came in after the ceremony and showed himself a real father, reminding me, in front of all the priests who were with him, of my visit to Bayeux and of my pilgrimage to Rome, without forgetting how I had put my hair up. Then taking my head in his hands, for a long time he made much of me.

Our Lord made me think of the caresses He would so soon be lavishing on me in front of all the Saints. What wonderful consolation it brought me, an inexpressible sweetness, like a foretaste of heavenly glory.

I have said that January 10 was Father's day of triumph! I liken that day to Palm Sunday and the entrance of Jesus into Jerusalem. Father's glory of a day was followed, like that of his Divine Master, by a sorrowful passion, and as the sufferings of Jesus pierced the heart of His Mother, so the sufferings and humiliations of the one we loved best on earth pierced ours.

I remember June, 1888; we feared he might have cerebral paralysis, and I surprised our Mistress by saying to her: "I am suffering very much, Mother, but I feel I can suffer yet more." I was not expecting at that time the trial which was in store for us; I did not know then that on February 12, only a month after my Clothing, Father would have so bitter a chalice to drink. I did not say I could suffer more when I knew that. I can find no words to express our anguish, and I am not going to try.

Later on, in Heaven, we will love to recall the dark days of exile, and indeed, even now, Father's three years of martyrdom seem to me the most desirable and fruitful years we have ever had, and I would not exchange them for the most sublime ecstasies. In face of such a priceless treasure, my heart cries out in gratitude: *"Blessed be Thou, my God, for the days wherein Thou hast afflicted us."* (Cf. *Ps.* 89:15).

Darling Mother, it was so bitter a cross, and yet

how precious and sweet, since drawing from our hearts such acts of love and gratitude; we no longer walked along the way of perfection—we ran.

Léonie and Céline were no longer of this world, though living in its midst. The letters they used to write at this period breathed a wonderful resignation, and I shall never forget Céline's visits. Far from keeping us apart, the bars of the grille only brought us closer together. We were animated by the same thoughts and desires, by the same love of Jesus and of souls; no word about earthly matters passed our lips. As before at Les Buissonnets, we winged our way, not only in thought but also in heart, beyond all space and time, and chose to suffer and to be despised on earth, that we might taste eternal happiness.

My desire for suffering was fully realized! Yet it lost none of its attraction, and it was not long before my soul had to share my heart's martyrdom.

My dryness increased. Both Heaven and earth denied me consolation; yet, though surrounded by the waters of tribulation which I sought so ardently, I was the happiest person in the world. I spent the time of betrothal like this, a betrothal which went on far longer than I would have wished, for even when my year was up, our Mother told me I must not dream of making my Profession yet, as the Superior was against it. I had to wait eight more months!

I found it hard to accept such a sacrifice at first, but before long my soul was flooded with divine light. I had been meditating on Surin's *Foundations of the Spiritual Life* and one day realized that my eagerness to take my vows was tainted with self-love.

If I really belonged to Jesus as His plaything, to console and entertain Him, it was for me to do what He wanted, not what I wanted. I realized, too, that a bride would not be very pleasing to her bridegroom on their wedding day unless she were beautifully arrayed, and I had done very little toward this.

So I told Our Lord: "I do not ask You to hasten my Profession any more. I'll wait as long as You like, but I'll make sure that our union is not delayed through any fault of mine. So I am going to work as hard as I can to make a bridal gown enriched with diamonds and jewels of every kind, and when it is lovely enough, I am sure You will let nothing stand in the way of making me Your bride."

I set to work with renewed zeal. Since taking the habit, I had already been given abundant light on religious perfection, and especially on the vow of poverty. When I was a postulant, I loved using nice things and having everything at hand when I needed it.

Jesus bore that patiently; He does not like teaching us everything at once, but normally enlightens us a little at a time.

At the beginning of my spiritual life, when I was between thirteen and fourteen, I used to wonder what else there was for me to learn. It did not seem possible that I could ever understand perfection any better than I already did. I soon found, however, that the more one advances, the further off one sees the goal to be.

I am quite resigned, now, to seeing myself always imperfect, and I even make it my joy.

To return to what Our Lord taught me: One day,

after Compline, I had searched in vain for our lamp on the shelves where it should have been; as it was the time of "Great Silence," I could do no more about it and thought, reasonably enough, that one of the Sisters had taken ours by mistake. But it meant my spending an hour in darkness, and just when I had calculated on doing a lot of work. I should certainly have complained about it without the light of grace, but as it was, instead of that, I rejoiced in the thought that poverty consisted in lacking not only little luxuries, but even things one could not do without. In the dark, I found my soul flooded with divine light.

At this period I developed a real love for the most ugly and inconvenient things; for example, I was delighted when I found that a dainty little jug in our cell had been replaced by a larger one, chipped all over.

I also tried not to make excuses, but found it very hard, especially where our Mistress was concerned, because I did not want to hide anything from her.

My first victory was not a very big one, but it cost me a great deal: someone or other had left a little vase on a window sill, and it was found broken. Our Mistress thought it was my fault. She seemed very annoyed that I had left it there and told me to be more careful next time, adding that I had no idea at all of tidiness. Without saying a word, I kissed the ground and promised I would take more care in the future. Such little things, as I have said, cost me a great deal because I was so lacking in virtue, and I had to remind myself that it would all be made known on the Day of Judgment.

I concentrated most of all on hidden acts of virtue; I used to like folding up the Sisters' choir mantles when they had forgotten them and would seek out a thousand ways of doing things for them.

I was also given an attraction to penance, though I was never allowed to indulge it. The only mortification which came my way was the mortification of self-love, but it did me much more good than corporal penances would have done.

Nevertheless, Our Lady was helping me to prepare a wedding garment for my soul, and as soon as it was finished, every obstacle disappeared. My Profession was fixed for September 8, 1890.

I really might have written many pages about all I have tried to say in so few words, but those pages will never be read on earth.

Chapter 8

PROFESSION AND
OBLATION TO MERCIFUL LOVE

NOW I must tell you about my retreat for Profession. Far from experiencing any consolation, complete aridity—desolation, almost—was my lot. Jesus was asleep in my little boat as usual. How rarely souls let Him sleep peacefully within them. Their agitation and all their requests have so tired out the Good Master that He is only too glad to enjoy the rest I offer Him. I do not suppose He will wake up until my eternal retreat, but instead of making me sad, it makes me very happy.

Such an attitude of mind proves that I am far from being a Saint. I should not rejoice in my aridity, but rather consider it as the result of lack of fervor and fidelity, while the fact that I often fall asleep during meditation, or while making my thanksgiving, should appall me. Well, I am not appalled; I bear in mind that little children are just as pleasing to their parents asleep as awake; that doctors put their patients to sleep while they perform operations, and that after all, *the Lord knoweth our frame. He remembereth that we are but dust.*" (*Ps.* 102:14).

My retreat for Profession, as I was saying, was spent in great aridity, as were those that followed, but without my being aware of it, the way to please God and practice virtue was being made clear to me. I have often noticed that Jesus will not give me a store of provisions; He nourishes me with food that is entirely new from moment to moment, and I find it in my soul without knowing how it got there. In all simplicity, I believe that Jesus Himself is, in a mysterious way, at work in the depths of my soul, inspiring me with whatever He wants me to do at that moment.

A few hours before my Profession, I received the precious blessing of the Holy Father, sent on from Rome by Bro. Simeon, and it certainly helped me to weather my life's most furious storm. The vigil preceding the dawn of one's Day of Profession is normally full of consolation; during mine, my vocation suddenly appeared to me nothing but a dream, some idle fancy. The devil . . . yes, it certainly was the devil . . . made me feel sure that I was quite unsuited for the Carmelite life and that I was only deceiving my Superiors by persisting in a life to which I was not called.

So deep became my darkness that one fact alone was clear to me—I did not have a religious vocation and must return to the world. My anguish was indescribable. What did one do in such a crisis? Only one thing: tell the Novice Mistress all about it at once. So I went and called her out of choir, and in great embarrassment, revealed the state of my soul. Luckily she could see things more clearly than I did; she only laughed at my fears and reassured me com-

pletely. Moreover, my act of humility acted like a
charm in putting the devil to flight. He had hoped
to catch me in his toils by getting me to keep my
trouble to myself. But it was I who caught him; I
completed my humiliation by revealing the whole
thing to Mother Prioress too, and her consoling reply
dispelled my doubts entirely.

The following morning, September 8, an outpouring of peace flooded my soul, that *"peace which
surpasseth all understanding"* (*Phil.* 4:7), and in this
peace I pronounced my sacred vows.

I asked for so many graces. I felt I really was a
queen, and I took advantage of my title to get all
the favors I could from the King for His ungrateful
subjects. I did not forget anyone. I wanted all the
sinners in the world to be converted that day, and
Purgatory emptied of every single captive. Close to
my heart I carried this letter, expressing all my own
desires:

"Jesus, my Divine Spouse, grant that I may ever
keep my baptismal robe spotless. Take me from this
world rather than let me tarnish my soul by one small
voluntary fault. May I seek and find You alone! May
no mortal creatures absorb my heart, nor I theirs!
May nothing in the world ever disturb my peace! O
Jesus, it is peace I beg of You. Peace, and above all,
boundless love. Jesus, let me die for You, a martyr;
grant me martyrdom of soul or of body, or better
still, grant me both! Grant that I may keep my vows
perfectly, that no one may trouble about me; that I
may be trampled underfoot, forgotten like a tiny grain
of sand. I offer myself to You, my Beloved, that You

may do in me everything You will, unhindered by any created obstacle."

At the close of this wonderful day, I laid my crown of roses, according to custom, at Our Lady's feet, and I did not feel sad, because it seemed to me that time could never dim my happiness. The Nativity of Mary! A beautiful feast on which to become the Spouse of Jesus. Our Lady, newly born, was giving her *little* flower to *Little* Jesus.

Everything was little that day, except the graces given to me, except my peace and joy at dusk, as I gazed upon the loveliness of a star-lit sky and thought that Heaven would claim me before very long, that there I should be united to my Divine Spouse, happy for all eternity.

I took the veil on September 24, and the day itself was veiled—veiled in sorrow, for Father was so ill that he could not come to bless his "little queen." At the last moment, Mgr. Hugonin, who was to have officiated, could not come either, and finally, so many other things went wrong that it all ended in sorrow and misery. Nevertheless at the bottom of my chalice there was peace, always peace.

That day, Jesus did nothing to help me to restrain my tears, and no one understood them. I know I had gone through far worse things than this before without crying, but only because I had had the help of great grace; whereas, Jesus left me to my own resources on September 24, and it was obvious that they were not enough.

Eight days after this, Jeanne Guérin, my cousin, was married to Dr. Néele, and the next time she was able to visit me, she told me all the countless things she did for her husband. I felt my heart thrill and thought: "No one shall say that a woman in the world does more for her husband who is merely mortal than I for my Beloved Jesus." Filled with fresh ardor, I set myself, as never before, to do everything to please my Heavenly Spouse, the King of Kings, who had chosen to honor me by a divine alliance.

Having seen the wedding invitations, I amused myself by making up the following invitation, which I read aloud to the novices. Something had struck me, and I wanted to bring it home to them: the glory of earthly unions cannot compare with the glory of being the Spouse of Jesus:

ALMIGHTY GOD
The Creator of Heaven & Earth
and Ruler of the World
and
THE MOST GLORIOUS VIRGIN MARY
Queen of the Court of Heaven
Invite you to the Spiritual Marriage of Their
August Son
JESUS, KING OF KINGS,
and LORD OF LORDS
with
Little Thérèse Martin,

now Lady and Princess of the Kingdoms of the Childhood and Passion of Jesus, given in dowry by her Divine Spouse, from whom she holds her titles of nobility: OF THE CHILD JESUS and OF THE HOLY FACE.

It was not possible to invite you to the Wedding Feast celebrated on Mount Carmel on September 8, 1890, only the Celestial Choir being admitted.

You are nevertheless invited to the Bride's RECEPTION tomorrow, the Day of Eternity, when Jesus, the Son of God, will come in splendor on the clouds of Heaven to judge the Living and the Dead.

The hour being uncertain, please hold yourself in readiness and watch.

*   *   *

That year the general retreat was a time of great grace. Normally I find a preached retreat very trying, and as I had suffered so much before, I fortified myself by a fervent novena. But this was different.

It was said that the Father was better at converting sinners than at directing religious. I must, then, be a great sinner, because God certainly used him to help me.

I had been undergoing all sorts of interior trials at this time, which I could not explain to anyone, yet here was someone who understood me perfectly, as though inspired by God, and my soul opened out completely. He launched me full sail upon that sea of confidence and love which had attracted me so much, but on which I had never dared to set out. He told me that my faults did not cause God sorrow and added: "At this moment I stand in His place, as far as you are concerned, and on His behalf I assure you that He is very satisfied with your soul."

How happy these consoling words made me! No one had ever told me before that faults did not pain

God; this assurance filled me with joy and made it possible to bear my exile patiently. My inmost thoughts had been echoed. For a long time I had felt sure that Our Lord was more tender than any mother, and I had sounded the depths of more than one mother's heart. I know from experience that a mother is always ready to forgive her child's little involuntary faults. No rebuke could have touched me half as much as a single kiss from you. Such is my nature that fear only keeps me back, while under the sway of love I not only advance—I fly!

Two months after this retreat, Mother Genevieve of St. Teresa, our Foundress, left the Carmel here for the Carmel of Heaven. Before I tell you my impressions at the time she died, I must tell you how fortunate I was to have lived for several years with a Saint whose example of simple and hidden virtue could be imitated.

There were many occasions when she gave me great consolation. One Sunday, for example, I went to see her in the infirmary and found two of the older Sisters with her. I was discreetly beating a retreat when she called me back, saying, as if in some way inspired: "Wait, my child, I have something to say to you. You are always asking for a spiritual bouquet; very well, today I give you this one: 'Serve God in peace and joy, and remember, our God is the God of Peace.'"

I thanked her simply and left in tears, convinced that God had revealed my state of soul to her, for I had been tried to such an extent that day that I was on the brink of despondency, and so great was my darkness that I did not even know whether or not

God still loved me. You can guess, Mother, what joy and peace replaced these shadows. The following Sunday I asked her what revelation she had had, but she assured me that she had received none at all. This only increased my respect for her, for I saw to what an extent Jesus was living in her soul, guiding her always. This seems to me the truest kind of holiness and the best; it is the kind of holiness I want because it is free from illusions.

The day her exile ended and she reached her homeland, I received a very special grace. I had never been present at a deathbed before; it is a most beautiful sight, but during my two-hour watch at the foot of the bed, I was overcome by drowsiness. I felt guilty about it, but at the very moment she entered Heaven, my state of soul was completely changed. In the twinkling of an eye, I was filled with joy, a joy I cannot describe. It was as if the saintly soul of our Foundress had at that moment given me a share in the happiness she enjoyed already, for I am sure she went straight to Heaven.

I had said to her once: "You won't go to Purgatory, Mother," and she had gently answered: "I hope not."

God certainly could not fail anyone so humble, and all the favors we received after her death are proof enough of that.

All the Sisters hastened to claim something of hers, and you know what I hold so dear, Mother. I noticed a tear drop glistening upon her lashes during her agony, like a lovely diamond. It was her last, and it never fell.

I saw it still sparkling as she was lying in state in

choir. That evening, when no one was looking, I was bold enough to go near with a little piece of linen, and now I am happy to possess a Saint's last tear.

I do not attach any importance to my dreams; besides, I rarely have any symbolic ones. I often wonder why I do not dream about God since I think about Him all day. My dreams are usually about woods, flowers, rivers and the sea. I am nearly always with children or chasing butterflies and birds I have never seen before; so you can see they are far from mystical, however poetic they may seem.

But one night after Mother Genevieve had died, I had one that was more consoling. I dreamed that she was giving each of us something which had belonged to her, and when my turn came, she was empty-handed. I thought there would be nothing for me, but she said three times, looking at me tenderly: "To you I leave my heart."

About a month after her death, so precious in God's sight, as 1891 was drawing to its close, an epidemic of influenza broke out in the community. Two other Sisters and I caught it only slightly, and were able to carry on. You cannot imagine the heartrending state of our Carmel during those days of mourning. The worst cases were looked after by others who could scarcely drag themselves about. Death reigned everywhere, and no sooner had a Sister breathed her last than she had to be left.

My nineteenth birthday was a sad one, for our sub-prioress died that day, and the infirmarian and I did what we could for her during her agony. Her death was soon followed by two more, and all the while I

was having to look after the sacristy by myself. I often
wondered how I managed to keep going.

One morning, when it was time to get up, I had
a presentiment that Sister Magdalene was no longer
alive. The corridor was in complete darkness, and no
one else had left her cell yet; but I decided to enter
hers. I found her lying fully dressed upon her mat-
tress in the stillness of death. I did not feel at all
frightened, and running to the sacristy at once, I
brought a blessed candle and set a crown of roses on
her head. The hand of God was here amid the desolation; His Heart was watching over us. The Sisters
passed effortlessly on from this life to the next with
the joy of Heaven on their faces and looked as though
quietly asleep.

During those trying weeks, I had the indescribable
happiness of going to Communion every day. How
wonderful it was! For a long time, Jesus was indul-
gent with me, far longer than He was with His more
faithful brides, for even when the epidemic was over,
He still came to me daily, without the community
sharing my good fortune. I had not sought this privilege, but what a supreme joy to be united to my
Beloved every day! I had the privilege, too, of han-
dling the sacred vessels and preparing the altar linen
to receive Our Lord. I felt that this should increase
my fervor, often calling to mind those words addressed
to the deacon: "Be ye holy, ye who carry the vessels
of the Lord." (*Ordination of a Deacon*).

But what shall I say of my thanksgivings, not only
at that time, but always? There is no time when I
feel less consolation, and that is natural enough,

because I desire Him to come for His own pleasure, not for mine.

I think of my soul as a piece of waste ground and ask Our Lady to take away the rubbish of my imperfections and then build a spacious tabernacle there, worthy of Heaven, adorning it with her own loveliness. Then I invite the Angels and the Saints to come and sing canticles of love; it seems to me that Jesus is glad to be magnificently received like this, and I share His joy.

But this does not keep distractions away, and I am often troubled by drowsiness, with the result that I resolve to continue my thanksgiving for the rest of the day, because I have made such a poor one in choir. As you can gather from this, Mother, my path is certainly not one of fear. Our Lord Himself encourages me to follow it, and I always know how to be happy and profit from my miseries.

I do not normally feel any anxiety when going to Holy Communion, but there was one occasion when I did. There had been a shortage of Hosts for several days, so that I had received only a small piece, and on this particular morning I most foolishly said to myself: "If I only receive part of a Host today, I will know that Jesus does not really want to come into my heart." I went up, and to my joy, after a moment's hesitation, the priest gave me *two complete Hosts*: what a lovely answer!

I have every reason, Mother, to be most grateful to God, and I am going to let you into another precious secret. He has shown the same mercy to me as He did to King Solomon. He has granted me every wish, not only my desires for perfection, but also for things which I knew were vanities, in theory at any rate, if not in practice.

You were always my ideal, and I wanted to be just like you; so, seeing you paint charming miniatures and write beautiful poetry, I thought how happy I would be if I, too, could paint, write poetry and do some good to those about me. Nevertheless, I did not like to ask for such natural gifts, and no one knew what desires lay hidden in the depths of my heart, except Jesus, who was hidden there too. He made use of this occasion to show me once again the nothingness of transitory things. Much to everyone's surprise, I had succeeded in painting several pictures, writing poetry and through Him helping several souls. But just as Solomon, "*turning to all the things which his hand had wrought, and to the labours wherein he had laboured in vain, saw in all things vanity and vexation of mind*" (*Eccles.* 2:11), so I learned by experience that true happiness on earth consists in being forgotten and in remaining completely ignorant of created things. I understood that all we accomplish, however brilliant, is worth nothing without love. Instead of doing me any harm, these gifts lavished upon me by Our Lord unite me even more closely to Him, for I realize that He alone is unchangeable and that He alone can satisfy the multitude of my desires.

While on the subject of these desires, I will tell you of another sort which He deigned to satisfy—childish ones, such as for snow on my Clothing Day. You know, Mother, what a love I had of flowers, and when I shut myself up at fifteen, I had renounced forever the joy of wandering through fields lovely with the treasures of spring, yet I never had so many flowers as I have had since I entered Carmel.

In the world, a fiancé always offers beautiful bouquets to his beloved, and Jesus did not forget about this. I received for His altar in abundance all the flowers that most delighted me: cornflowers and poppies and big daisies; yet amidst all these, there was one small friend who was not in the company—the corncockle. I did so want to see it again, and not so long ago it came too, all smiling, to prove to me that in little things, as much as in big ones, God gives even in this life a hundredfold to those who have left everything for love of Him.

Only one desire remained, my fondest, and with good reason the most unrealizable: that Céline should enter the Carmel of Lisieux. I had, however, sacrificed this desire and left my darling sister's future solely in the hands of God. Though I was prepared to see her go off, if necessary, to the ends of the earth, I longed to see her like myself, the Spouse of Christ; and to see her exposed in the world to dangers I had never known was a source of great suffering to me. My feelings in regard to her were rather those of a mother than of a sister, full of loving solicitude for her soul.

Once, when she was going to a ball with my aunt and my cousins, for some unknown reason, I felt unusually anxious, so much so that, in a torrent of tears, I begged Our Lord to prevent her dancing. My prayer was answered literally! Normally she danced most gracefully, but the future bride of Christ could not dance that evening, while her partner shared her fate, finding it impossible to do more than walk very solemnly backwards and forwards with her, to everyone's great astonishment. This embarrassed the unfortunate young man so much that he vanished and did not dare show himself again for the rest of the evening.

This unique incident greatly increased my confidence and proved quite clearly that Jesus had already set His seal upon my darling sister's brow.

He called Father to Himself last year, on July 29—Father, who had gone through such trials and was so saintly. Uncle had looked after him most carefully during his last two years and lightened his sorrows with every kind of attention. But all this while, Father was so infirm and helpless that we saw him only once at visiting time. How sad that interview was, as I expect you remember, Mother! When it was time to go and we were saying goodbye, he raised his eyes and remained for a long time pointing to Heaven. He did not need to say anything, only one phrase in a voice choked with tears: "In Heaven!"

Heaven, with all its wonders, is now his; the ties which bound his guardian angel to earth are broken, for angels do not remain here below once their task is done. They wing their way back to God. That is why they have wings, and that is why Céline tried to fly off to Carmel. But the difficulties seemed insuperable.

One morning, when her affairs were getting more tangled than ever, I said to Our Lord after Communion:

"You know, my Jesus, how much I have desired that Father's trials should count as his Purgatory. I long to know if this desire has been fulfilled. I do not ask You to tell me Yourself; I only ask for a sign. You know the attitude of Sister X to Céline's entering, and I will take it as a sign that Father has gone straight to Heaven if she no longer raises objections."

How infinite is God's mercy! How ineffable His condescension! He who holds the hearts of His creatures in the palm of His hand and fashions them as He wills changed this Sister's heart. She was the very first person I met after finishing my thanksgiving. She called me over, and there were tears in her eyes as she spoke to me about Céline's entering, and it was obvious that she was really eager to have her with us.

It was not long before the Bishop removed the last obstacle and without any hesitation allowed you, Mother, to open our doors to the little exiled dove.

My only desire now is to love Jesus even to folly. Yes, I am drawn by love alone, no longer desiring suffering or death, yet both are dear to me, and for a long time now I have looked on them as harbingers of joy. I have suffered and thought I had reached the shores of Heaven. Ever since I was very young, I have been convinced that the little flower would be gathered in the springtime of her life; now I am guided by self-abandonment alone and need no other compass, no longer knowing how to ask for anything with eagerness except that God may do His will completely in my soul. I can truly say what our father, St. John of the Cross, says in his Canticle:

Deeply I drank in the inner cellar
Of the One I love.
And all this plain was strange to me
And all my flocks were lost to me
When I came forth again.
I gave my soul and all I have to Him.
No longer do I shepherd sheep;
No other task for me
Save only love.
—*Spiritual Canticle,* stanzas 26 & 28

Yet more:

Since I have known the rule of Love,
It has so mastered me
That all the good and ill in me
Serves Love's own end.
Love turns my soul to Love itself.
—*Hymn to the Deity*

How sweet the way of Love, Mother! One can fall, I know; there may be infidelities, yet Love knows how *to turn all things to profit,* quickly consuming everything which might displease Jesus, and leaving at the bottom of one's heart nothing but deep and humble peace.

The works of St. John of the Cross have been such a source of light to me. Between the ages of sixteen and eighteen, I read no one else. Later on, spiritual writers always left me cold, and still do. Whenever I open a book, no matter how beautiful or touching, my heart dries up, and I can understand nothing of what I read; or, if I do understand, my mind will go no further, and I cannot meditate. I am rescued from this helpless state by the Scriptures and *The Imitation*, finding in them a hidden manna, pure and substantial; but during meditation I am sustained above all else by the Gospels. They supply my poor soul's every need, and they are always yielding up to me new lights and mysterious hidden meanings. I know from experience that "*the Kingdom of God is within us*" (*Luke* 17:21), that Jesus has no need of books or doctors to instruct our soul; He, the Doctor of Doctors, teaches us without the sound of words. I have never heard Him speak, and yet I know He is within my soul. Every moment He is guiding and inspiring me, and just at the moment I need them, "lights" till then unseen are granted me. Most often it is not at prayer that they come, but while I go about my daily duties.

So many graces, Mother! May I not sing with the Psalmist that "*the Lord is good, that His mercy endureth forever*"? (*Ps.* 117:1). It seems to me that if everyone received such graces, no one would dread Him, but love Him with an *unbounded love*; for it is love rather than fear which leads us to avoid the smallest voluntary fault.

But then I realized that we cannot all be alike; there must be different kinds of holiness to glorify the divine perfections. To me He has manifested His Infinite Mercy, and it is in this shining mirror that I gaze upon His other attributes, which there appear all radiant with love—all, even justice.

What joy to remember that Our Lord is just, that He makes allowances for all our shortcomings and knows full well how weak we are. What have I to fear then? Surely the God of infinite justice, who pardons the Prodigal Son with such mercy, will be *just* with me "*who am always with him*"? (Cf. *Luke* 15:31).

It was in 1895 that I received the grace to understand more than ever before how much Jesus longs for us to love Him. One day I was thinking about those who offer themselves as victims to God's justice, diverting to themselves the punishments deserved by sinners. The nobility and generosity of such an offering was obvious, yet I myself was far from being drawn to make it, and from the bottom of my heart I cried:

"O my Divine Master, is it only Your Justice that shall find atoning victims? Surely Your Merciful Love has need of victims too? It is rejected and ignored on every side; the hearts on which You long to lavish it turn towards earthly creatures, seeking their happiness in a momentary affection, instead of running to Your arms to be consumed in the enrapturing furnace of Your Infinite Love. O my God, must Your Love remain disdained forever in Your Heart? It seems to me that if You found souls offering themselves to Your Love as holocausts, You would consume them speedily, rejoicing that the rays of infinite tenderness had no longer to be imprisoned in Your Heart. If Your Justice must be satisfied, although it extends only to earth, surely Your Merciful Love must long far more to fire our souls, because '*Thy Mercy reacheth even to the Heavens.*' (*Ps.* 35:6). O Jesus, grant me to be Your happy victim; consume me in the fire of Divine Love, Your little holocaust."

You, Mother, who permitted me to make the offering of myself to God, you know what flames of love, what a sea of grace, filled my soul the moment I had made my *Act of Oblation* on June 9, 1895.

And since that day, love has surrounded me and penetrated me through and through. Moment by moment, the Merciful Love of God renews and cleanses me and leaves my heart without a trace of sin. Purgatory holds no fears for me; I know I do not deserve even to enter this place of expiation with the Holy Souls. But I also know that the Fire of Love is far more sanctifying than the fires there; I know that Jesus cannot want us to suffer uselessly and that He would not fill me with the desires I feel if He did not mean to grant them.

This, my darling Mother, is all I am able to tell you of the life of your Thérèse. Deep in your heart you know her better than she knows herself; you know what Jesus has done for her and so will pardon me for having cut short the story of her religious life.

The story of the "little white flower"! How will it end? Perhaps the "little flower" will be gathered while still fresh, or be transplanted to some other shore; who knows?

One thing I know: God's Mercy will go with her always, and she will never cease to bless the Mother who gave her to Jesus. She will eternally rejoice to be a flower in her crown; with her she will eternally sing the canticle of love and gratitude that is ever new.

Chapter 9

LIFE IN CARMEL

DEAR Reverend Mother, you have expressed the desire that I should sing "*the mercies of the Lord*" (*Ps.* 88:1) to the end. I am not going to argue with you about it, but I cannot help smiling as I take up my pen again to tell you what you know as well as I do. I will simply do as I am told.

I do not seek to know what use this manuscript could be and have no hesitation in saying, Mother, that I should not be in the least worried if you burned it before my eyes without even reading it.

The general opinion of the Community is that you have thoroughly spoiled me since the day I entered Carmel, but "*Man seeth those things that appear, but the Lord beholdeth the heart.*" (*1 Kings* 16:7).

I thank you, Mother, for not having spared me; Jesus knew very well that His little flower was so frail that without the life-giving waters of humiliation she would never take root; and this priceless blessing she owes to you.

For some months now, the Divine Master has completely changed His way of dealing with His little flower: doubtless because He thinks she has been watered quite enough already, He allows her to unfold in the warmth of the bright sun. He only smiles upon her now, and she owes this, too, to you, Reverend Mother.

Far from withering her, this lovely sunlight only serves to make her grow most beautifully. In her calix, she treasures the precious drops of dew she once received, and they will always remind her of her littleness and weakness. Everyone can stoop to admire her, can shower praise upon her without its casting a shadow of vain-glory upon the true happiness in her heart, the happiness she feels in knowing that she is no more than a worthless little thing in the eyes of God.

When I say that compliments have no effect upon me, Mother, I am not referring to the love and confidence you have shown me; that, on the contrary, touches me deeply, but I feel that I need not be afraid of praise anymore and can enjoy it in all simplicity, attributing all that is good in me to the goodness of God.

If it pleases Him to make me appear better than I am, that is no concern of mine. He is free to do just as He likes. How different are the ways by which You guide our souls, my God!

We find in the lives of the Saints that many of them, when they died, left nothing by which we might remember them, and no writings at all. Yet there are others, like our Holy Mother St. Teresa, who have enriched the Church with their wonderful works, who were not afraid "*to make known the secrets of the King*" (Cf. *Tob.* 12:7), that He may be the better known and loved.

Which of these two ways is more pleasing to Our Lord? It seems to me He finds both equally pleasing.

All these friends of God have followed the guidance of the Holy Spirit, who inspired the Prophet to write: "*Tell the just man that all is well.*" (Cf. *Is.* 3:10). Yes, all is well when one seeks nothing but the Divine Will; that is why the little flower obeys Jesus by trying to please those who hold His place on earth.

You know that I have always wanted to be a Saint; but compared with real Saints, I know perfectly well that I am no more like them than a grain of sand trodden beneath the feet of passers-by is like a mountain with its summit lost in the clouds.

Instead of allowing this to discourage me, I say to myself: "God would never inspire me with desires which cannot be realized; so, in spite of my littleness, I can hope to be a Saint. I could never grow up. I must put up with myself as I am, full of imperfections, but I will find a little way to Heaven, very short and direct, an entirely new way.

"We live in the age of inventions now, and the wealthy no longer have to take the trouble to climb the stairs; they take an elevator. That is what I must find, *an elevator* to take me straight up to Jesus, because I am too little to climb the steep stairway of perfection."

So, I searched the Scriptures for some hint of my desired *elevator*, until I came upon these words from the lips of Eternal Wisdom: "*Whosoever is a little one, let him come to Me.*" (Prov. 9:4). I went closer to God, feeling sure that I was on the right path, but as I wanted to know what He would do to a "little

one," I continued my search. This is what I found:
"*You shall be carried at the breasts and upon the knees;
as one whom the mother caresseth, so will I comfort
you.*" (*Is.* 66:12, 13). My heart had never been moved
by such tender and consoling words before!

Your arms, My Jesus, are the elevator which will take
me up to Heaven. There is no need for me to grow
up; on the contrary, I must stay little, and become
more and more so.

O God, You have gone beyond my dreams, and
I—I only want to sing Your mercies!

"*Thou hast taught me, O Lord, from my youth, and
till now I have declared Thy wonderful works, and shall
do so unto old age and grey hairs.*" (Cf. *Ps.* 70:17, 18).

When shall I reach old age? It seems to me it might
just as well be now as later, for in Your eyes, two
thousand years are but a single day!

Do not think that your child wants to leave you,
thinking that it is better to die at dawn than at dusk.
It is because she only wants to please Jesus. Now that
He seems to be coming to take her home to Heaven,
she is happy at heart; she knows full well that God
can do good on earth without the help of anyone—
of her least of all.

I know what you want me to do while waiting:
you want me to finish the delightful and easy work
you have given me to do at your side, a work which
I will complete from Heaven. You have said to me
what Jesus said to St. Peter: "*Feed my lambs.*" (*John*
21:15). I must say I am very surprised, for I am much
too little. I begged you to feed them yourself and to
number me among your flock. It was a reasonable

request, and you did not entirely refuse it. You made me, not their Novice Mistress, but the senior novice, telling me to lead them to fertile and shady pastures, to point out the best and most nourishing grass, and warn them about those poisonous flowers which look so attractive but which they must never touch, save to crush them underfoot.

Why were you not afraid of my youth and inexperience? What if I should lead your lambs astray? Perhaps you remembered that it often pleases God to give wisdom to little ones.

There are so few people who do not make their own limited understanding the measure of God's power. They admit that there may be exceptions here below, but God has no right to make them! I know it has been the custom for a long time to measure experience by years. In his youth, David sang to the Lord, "*I am young and despised*" (*Ps*. 118:141), yet in the very same Psalm he does not fear to say, "*I have had understanding above old men because I have sought Thy commandments; Thy word is a lamp to my feet and a light to my paths; I have sworn and I am determined to keep the judgments of Thy justice.*" (*Ps.* 118:100, 105, 106). You did not even consider it imprudent to tell me, one day, that the Divine Master was enlightening me, and it was as though I had had years of experience.

I am too little, now, to be vain, too little to know how to coin fine phrases indicating how very humble I am. I prefer to say quite simply: "*He that is mighty has done great things to me*" (*Luke* 1:49), and the greatest thing He has done is to show me how insignificant I am and how incapable of doing any good.

I have experienced tribulations of all sorts and suffered a great deal. When I was a child, suffering used to make me sad; now I taste its bitterness with joy and peace.

I must admit that you would have to know me very well not to smile as you read this. No one seems less tried than I am, yet how surprised you would all be if only you knew the martyrdom I have suffered this last year. You want me to tell you about it, so I am going to try, but there are no words for things like this, and I shall always fall short of the reality.

Last year, during Lent, I felt stronger than ever, and I noticed that I lost none of my energy until Easter, in spite of keeping the full fast. But in the early hours of Good Friday, Jesus gave me cause to hope that I would be joining Him in Heaven before long. The very memory of that moment is delightful!

I had not been given permission to watch all night at the Altar of Repose, and so I had retired to our cell at midnight. I had scarcely laid my head upon the pillow, when I felt a burning stream rise to my lips. Nevertheless, as I had already put out our lamp, I restrained my curiosity and slept peacefully until the morning.

The rising bell rang at five o'clock, and at once I remembered that there was some good news awaiting me. I went over to the window, and it was good news; our handkerchief was drenched in blood. I was filled with hope, convinced that my Beloved, on the anniversary of His death, had let me hear His first call—a far-off lovely murmur, heralding His approach.

I assisted at Prime and at Chapter with much fervor, then hurried to kneel before you and tell you of my happiness. I did not feel the least tiredness or pain and easily obtained permission to finish Lent as I had begun. Good Friday found me taking my full share of all our austerities, and they had never seemed so dear to me. I was filled with joy. I was going to Heaven.

That evening I retired to our cell, still full of joy, and once more slept peacefully, though Jesus again gave me the same sign of my approaching entry into Eternal Life.

My faith was so strong and vivid that the thought of Heaven made me supremely happy. It seemed impossible that anyone could be so wicked as to have no faith. They could not possibly be sincere in denying the existence of another world.

During the radiant days of Paschaltide, Jesus taught me that there really are souls who by their abuse of grace have lost the precious treasures of faith and hope, and with them all joy that is pure and true. He allowed my soul to be enveloped in utter darkness. Ever since I was very little, the thought of Heaven had always been a joy to me; now it brought torment and conflict.

This trial did not last merely a few days or weeks; it went on for months, and I am still waiting to be delivered from it. It is impossible to explain what I feel—I only wish I could. I am in a dark tunnel, and you would have to go through it yourself to understand how dark it is, but a comparison may give you some idea.

Suppose I had been born in a land which was always deep in fog; I should never have seen the beauties of nature, never a ray of sunlight. But from my childhood I should have heard about them, should have known I was in exile, and that there was another land I was bound to seek. The inhabitants of the land of fog have not made up this story; it is absolutely true, for the King of the Land of Sunshine came to spend thirty-three years here: but *"the darkness did not understand that He was the light of the world."* (Cf. *John* 1:5).

But Your child, O Lord, has understood. She asks pardon for her brothers who do not believe. She is quite content to eat the bread of sorrow as long as You will her to. For love of You, she will sit at this table laden with the bitter food of sinners and will not rise until You give the sign. Yet in their name and in her own, may she not say: *"O God, be merciful to us sinners"*? (Cf. *Luke* 18:13). Send us away justified. May all in whom the light of faith shines dimly see at last. If the table they have defiled must be purified by one who loves You, I am willing to sit there alone eating nothing but the bread of tears until You choose to take me into Your Kingdom of Light. I ask only one grace—may I never offend You."

Since childhood, as I said, I had been certain that one day I would leave my dark world far behind. I do not think that this was only from what I had heard. The very desires and intuitions of my inmost heart assured me that another and more lovely land awaited me, an abiding city—just as the genius of Christopher Columbus gave him a presentiment of a new world.

Then suddenly the fog about me seems to enter my very soul and fill it to such an extent that I cannot even find there the lovely picture I had formed of my homeland; everything has disappeared!

When, weary of being enveloped by nothing but darkness, I try to comfort and encourage myself with the thought of the eternal life to come, it only makes matters worse. The very darkness seems to echo the voices of those who do not believe and mocks at me: "You dream of light and of a fragrant land; you dream that the Creator of this loveliness will be your own for all eternity; you dream of escaping one day from these mists in which you languish! Dream on, welcome death; it will not bring you what you hope; it will bring an even darker night, the night of nothingness!"

This picture of my trial is no more than a rough sketch compared with the reality, but I dare not say more for fear it might be blasphemy! Perhaps I have said too much already? God forgive me, but He knows that I try to practice my faith, even though it brings me no joy. I have made more acts of faith in the last year than during all the rest of my life.

Whenever I find myself faced with the prospect of an attack by my enemy, I am most courageous; I turn my back on him, without so much as looking at him, and run to Jesus. I tell Him I am ready to shed all my blood to prove my faith in Heaven. I tell Him I am quite happy that the eyes of my soul should be blind, while I am on earth, to the heavenly wonders in store for me, so long as He will open the eyes of unbelieving souls for all eternity. So, in spite of the fact that this trial takes away all sense of joy, I can still say: "*Thou hast given me, O Lord, a delight in Thy doings*" (*Ps.* 91:5), for what can give such keen delight as suffering for love of You! The more personal the suffering and the more hidden from the eyes of the world, the more pleasing it is to You, my God.

If, to suppose the impossible, You did not know about it, I would be no less happy to suffer, hoping that I might, by my tears, prevent a single sin against the Faith, or at least atone for it.

I expect you will think I am rather exaggerating the night of my soul; to judge by the poems I have written this year, I must appear to be overwhelmed with consolation, a child for whom the veil of faith is almost torn apart; yet it is no longer a veil—it is a wall reaching almost to Heaven, shutting out the stars.

When I sing of Heaven's happiness, of what it is to possess God forever, I feel no joy; I simply sing of what I want to believe. Now and then, I must admit, a gleam of light shines through the dark night to bring a moment's respite, but afterwards, its memory, instead of consoling me, only makes my night darker than ever.

Yet I realize as never before that the Lord is gentle and merciful; He did not send me this heavy cross until I could bear it. If He had sent it before, I am certain that it would have discouraged me, but now it merely takes away from me any natural satisfaction I might feel in longing for Heaven.

It seems to me at the moment that there is nothing to prevent my flying away, because I desire nothing at all now except to love until I die of love. I am free, I am not afraid of anything, not even of what I used to dread most of all . . . a long illness which would make me a burden to the community.

I am perfectly content to go on suffering in body and soul for years, if that would please God. I am not in the least afraid of living for a long time; I am ready to go on fighting.

The Lord is the rock upon which I stand. "*He teaches my hands to fight and my fingers to war. He is my Protector, and I have hoped in Him.*" (Cf. *Ps.* 143:1, 2).

I have never asked God to let me die young; true, I have never ceased to believe that I shall, but I have never sought it in any way. God often asks no more than the desire to work for His glory—and you know the extent of my desires! You know, too, that Jesus has offered me more than one bitter chalice through my sisters.

David had good reason to sing: "*Behold how good and how pleasant it is for brethren to dwell together in unity.*" (*Ps.* 132:1). But this unity is impossible on earth without sacrifice.

I did not come to Carmel to be with my sisters; on the contrary, I saw clearly that their presence would cost me dearly, for I was determined not to give way to nature. How can anyone say that it is more perfect to cut oneself off from one's family? Has anyone ever blamed brothers for fighting side by side in battle and for winning the palm of martyrdom together? It is no doubt true that they encourage one another, but the martyrdom of one affects them all.

It is the same in the religious life, which theologians call a martyrdom. A heart given to God loses none of its natural tenderness; on the contrary, the more pure and divine it becomes, the more such tenderness increases.

Such is the affection with which I love you, Mother, and my sisters. I am glad to fight side by side with them for the glory of the King of Heaven; but at the same time, I should be quite ready to go and fight on another battlefield, should the Divine General so wish. No command would be necessary, a look or a sign would be enough.

Since entering Carmel, I have always thought that if Jesus did not carry me off to Heaven quickly, I should share the lot of Noah's dove; He would open the window of the Ark one day and would bid me fly away to distant pagan shores bearing the olive branch. I have soared above all earthly things at the very thought!

Knowing that even in Carmel there can be separations, I have tried to make Heaven my home even now; I have accepted exile among an unknown people, not only for myself, but—a far more bitter thing—for my sisters too.

Two of them were, in fact, asked for by our daughter-house in Saigon, and for some time the matter was considered seriously. I would not have said a single word to hold them back, although the thought of what awaited them nearly broke my heart. There is no question of that now. The Superiors have placed insurmountable obstacles in the way; my lips touched the chalice only long enough to taste its bitterness.

Let me tell you why I want to respond to the appeal from Hanoi if Our Lady cures me. To live in a Carmel abroad, it seems that one must have a very special vocation, and many are mistaken in thinking themselves called to it, but you have told me I am called, my health being the only obstacle. If I do one day have to leave the cradle of my religious life, it will not be without a pang; my heart is very sensitive, and because of this, I want to offer Jesus every kind of suffering it can bear.

I am loved here, by you and by my Sisters, and this love is dear to me; that is why I dream of a convent where I should be unknown, where I should have to suffer exile of heart as well.

I should leave everything I love so much, not because I think I would be useful there in Hanoi— I know too well how useless I am—but simply to do God's Will and to sacrifice myself for Him in any way which will please Him.

I am sure I should not be disappointed; the smallest joy is a surprise when one expects nothing but pure suffering, and the very suffering becomes a supreme joy when sought as a priceless treasure.

I am ill, and I shall never get better, but my soul always remains at peace. For a long time now I have not belonged to myself; I have given myself entirely to Jesus. He is free to do with me whatever He likes.

He has given me a longing for complete exile and asked me if I were willing to drink that chalice, but as soon as I reached out my hand, the chalice was withdrawn. That was all He had wanted; my willingness was enough.

From what troubles we are saved, my God, by the vow of obedience! The simple religious, guided by the will of her Superiors alone, has the joy of being sure that she is on the right path; even when she is sure that her Superiors are mistaken, she need not fear.

But the moment she ceases to consult this infallible compass, she goes astray down barren pathways, where the waters of grace soon fail her.

You, Mother, are the compass which Jesus has given me to guide me safely to the eternal shore. To fulfill the will of God, I have only to keep my eyes on you. By allowing me to endure temptations against faith, the Divine Master has greatly increased in my heart *the spirit of faith,* which makes me see Him dwelling in your soul and directing me through you.

You certainly make the yoke of obedience sweet and light, but my dispositions are such that I am sure that even if you were to treat me harshly, I would not act in any other way, or lose any of my filial devotion. I should see even this as God's Will manifesting itself in yet another way for the greater good of my soul.

I have received countless graces this year, but the one I value most is the one of understanding the precept of charity in all its fullness. I had never fully understood before what Our Lord meant when He said: "*The second commandment is like to the first. Thou shalt love thy neighbor as thyself.*" (*Matt.* 22:39).

I had concentrated on loving God, but in loving Him, I came to realize the meaning of those other words of His: "*Not everyone that saith to Me, Lord, Lord, shall enter into the Kingdom of Heaven, but he that doth the will of My Father.*" (Cf. *Matt.* 7:21).

Now Jesus made known to me His Will at the Last Supper, when He gave His Apostles His *New Commandment: "Love one another as I have loved you.*" (*John* 13:34). I set to work to discover how Jesus had loved them. I found that He had not loved them for their natural qualities, for they were ignorant and taken up with earthly things, yet he called them *His friends* (*John* 15:15) and *His brothers* (*John* 20:17) and wanted to have them with Him in His Father's Kingdom; He was ready to die on the Cross to make this possible, saying: "*Greater love than this no man hath, that a man lay down his life for his friends.*" (*John* 15:13).

Meditating on these divine words, I saw only too well how very imperfect was my love for my Sisters; I did not really love them as Jesus loves them.

I see now that true charity consists in bearing with the faults of those about us, never being surprised at their weaknesses, but edified at the least sign of virtue. I see above all that charity must not remain hidden in the bottom of our hearts, for "*no man lighteth a candle and putteth it in a hidden place, nor under a bushel; but upon a candlestick, that they who come in may see the light.*" (*Luke* 11:33). It seems to me that this candle is the symbol of charity; it must shine out not only to cheer those we love best, but *ALL those who are of the household.*

Under the Old Law, when God told His people that they must love their neighbor as themselves, it was before He had come upon earth Himself; knowing how much man loved himself, it was the best He could ask. But when Jesus gives His Apostles a *New Commandment* (*John* 13:34), *His own Commandment* (*John* 15:12), He asks them to love one another, not only as they love themselves, but as He Himself loves them and will love them even unto the consummation of the world!

Yet I know, my Jesus, that You never command the impossible; You know better than I do how frail and imperfect I am; You know perfectly well that I can never hope to love my Sisters as You love them, unless You Yourself love them in me.

It is only because You are willing to do this that You have given us a *New* Commandment, and I love it because it is my assurance of Your desire to love in me all those whom You command me to love.

I know that whenever I am charitable, it is Jesus alone who is acting through me and that the more closely I unite myself to Him, the more I will be able to love all my Sisters.

Should the devil draw my attention to the faults of any one of them when I am seeking to increase this love in my heart, I call to mind at once her virtues and her good intentions. I tell myself that though I may have seen her fall once, there are probably a great many other occasions on which she has won victories which, in her humility, she has kept to herself. What may appear to me to be a fault may even be an act of virtue because of her intention,

and as I have experienced this for myself, I have little difficulty in persuading myself that this is indeed
the case.

It was one day during recreation. The Portress came
to ask one of us to help her in some particular duty.
I was as eager as a child to do this work, and as it
happened, I was chosen. Though I began to put away
my needlework at once, I did so sufficiently slowly
to give my neighbor a chance of folding hers first,
because I knew she would be glad to take my place.

The Portress noticed that I was taking my time,
and said laughingly: "I did not think you would add
this pearl to your crown: you were much too slow."
The whole community was left with the impression
that I had acted according to nature.

I cannot tell you what I gained from this incident
and how tolerant it made me. Praise is no longer an
occasion of vanity. I have only to say to myself: "If
my little acts of virtue can be mistaken for imperfections, imperfections can just as easily be mistaken
for virtue"; and I say with St. Paul: *'To me it is a
very small thing to be judged by you, or by man's day.
But neither do I judge myself. He that judgeth me is
the Lord.'"* (*1 Cor.* 4:3, 4).

I too am judged by the Lord; I am judged by Jesus.
I will never think uncharitably of anyone so that He
may judge me leniently, or rather, not at all, for He
has said: "*Judge not, and ye shall not be judged.*" (*Luke*
6:37).

I turned to the Gospels again where Our Lord
explains clearly His *New Commandment*: "*You have
heard that it hath been said, Thou shalt love thy neigh-*

bor and hate thy enemy: but I say unto you, Love your enemies and pray for them that persecute you." (*Matt.* 6:43, 44).

Of course, we have no enemies in Carmel, but we do have to contend with our natural feelings; one Sister attracts us, while we would go out of our way to avoid meeting another. Jesus tells me that it is this very Sister I must love; I must pray for her, even though she shows no sign of loving me. "*If you love them that love you, what thanks are to you? For sinners also love those that love them.*" (*Luke* 6:32).

A love which does not prove itself in action is not enough, nor is our natural readiness to please a friend; that is not charity, for sinners are ready to do the same. Jesus also teaches me to "*give to everyone that asketh thee; and of him that taketh away thy goods, ask them not again.*" (*Luke* 6:30). It is much harder to give to all who ask than to offer our services spontaneously; nor is it so hard to comply with a friendly request, but if we happen to be asked in a tactless way, we are at once up in arms, unless we are rooted in perfect charity. We find countless excuses, and only after we have made it quite clear to the Sister that she is lacking in courtesy, do we condescend to grant her request *as a favor*, or we do something for her which probably takes a twentieth of the time wasted in making excuses and insisting on our imaginary rights.

If it is hard to give to everyone who asks, it is harder still to let them take things away from us without asking for them back again. I say it is hard; I should rather say it seems hard, for "*the yoke of the*

Lord is sweet and His burden light" (Cf. *Matt.* 11:30), and as soon as we accept it, we realize that. The fact that Jesus does not want me to ask for anything back should seem to me natural enough, since nothing I have really belongs to me. I ought to rejoice when I have to put my vow of poverty into practice.

I used to think I was detached from everything, but now that I understand these words of Jesus, I realize how imperfect I am.

If, for example, I find my brushes all over the place when starting to paint, or if a ruler or penknife has disappeared, I have to take strong hold of myself to resist demanding them back with asperity. As I really need them, there is no harm in asking, and I am not going against what Jesus asks if I do so in all humility; on the contrary, I am only acting like the poor, who hold out their hands for alms and are not surprised if they are refused because nobody owes them anything. What peace floods a soul when it soars above natural feelings! The joy of the truly poor in spirit is beyond all compare; when they ask disinterestedly for something they need, and not only is it refused, but what they already have is taken away, they follow Our Lord's advice: "*If any man take away thy coat, let go thy cloak also unto him.*" (*Matt.* 5:40).

To surrender our cloak, so it seems to me, is to surrender our last rights, to consider ourselves as everyone's servant and slave.

When we have given away our coat, we can walk more easily, we can run, so Jesus adds: "*and whosoever will force thee one mile, go with him another two.*" (Matt. 5:41).

It is not even enough for me to give to all who ask; I must go beyond their desires and show myself very honored and only too glad to offer my services. If something which I normally use is taken away, I should appear happy to be *rid* of it.

I cannot always carry out these words of the Gospel to the letter; there are bound to be times when I have to refuse my Sisters something. But when we are deeply rooted in charity, we can always find a way to refuse so charmingly that our refusal gives more pleasure than the gift would have done.

It is true that we are more ready to ask those who are obviously more ready to oblige; nevertheless, we must never avoid those who ask for help too readily, on the pretext of having to refuse, for our Divine Master has said: "*From him that would borrow of thee, turn not away.*" (*Matt.* 5:42).

Nor should I show myself willing for the sake of appearances or in the hope of receiving some service in return, for Our Lord has also said: "*If you lend to them of whom you hope to receive, what thanks are to you? For sinners also lend to sinners for to receive as much. But you, do good and lend, hoping for nothing thereby, and your reward shall be great.*" (*Luke* 6:34, 35).

The reward certainly is great, even here on earth; and it is only the first step along this path that is difficult.

It seems hard *to lend, hoping to receive nothing*; it is much easier to *give outright*, for once we have given anything away, it no longer belongs to us.

When someone comes to us and says, full of assurance: "I need your help for a few hours, but don't worry, Reverend Mother has given permission, and I will repay the time you lend me," we know perfectly well that she never will and feel very much like saying: "I will *give* you the time"; it would gratify our self-love, for it is so much more generous to give than merely to lend, and we would make her feel that we do not think much of her services. The divine teaching certainly goes against our natural feelings, and without the help of grace, we could not even understand it, let alone put it into practice.

I feel that I am explaining myself worse than ever, and I cannot conceive what interest you could possibly find in reading this confused medley of thoughts; however, I am not striving for literary effect, and if my discourse on charity bores you, at least it is a proof of my goodwill.

I must admit that I am far from doing what I know I ought to do, but the very desire to do so brings me peace. If I happen to fall into some fault against charity, I get up again at once; for some months now, I have not even had to struggle.

I can say with St. John of the Cross, "My house is entirely at peace" (*Canticle*, strophe I), and I attribute this peace to a certain victory I gained. Since then, the hosts of Heaven have taken my part; they are not going to allow me to be wounded after having fought so bravely.

There was at that time a certain nun who managed to irritate me in everything she did. The devil had a part in it, for it was certainly he who made me see all her bad points. Not wishing to give way

to natural antipathy, I reminded myself that senti-
ments of charity were not enough; they must find
expression, and I set myself to treat her as if I loved
her best of all.

I prayed for her whenever we met, and offered all
her virtues and merits to God. I was sure that Jesus
would be delighted at this, for artists always like to
have their work praised, and it pleases the Divine
Artist of souls when, not stopping at the exterior, we
penetrate the inner sanctuary where He dwells, to
admire its beauty.

I prayed earnestly for this Sister who had caused
me so much struggle, but this was not enough for
me. I tried to do everything I possibly could for her,
and when tempted to answer her sharply, I hastened
to give her a friendly smile and talk about something
else, for, as it says in *The Imitation*, "It is better to
leave everyone to his own way of thinking than begin
an argument." (*Imit.*, III, xliv, 1).

Sometimes, when the devil made a particularly vio-
lent attack, if I could slip away without letting her
suspect my inward struggle, I would run away from
the battle *like a deserter*; and what was the result?

She said to me one day, her face radiant: "What
do you find so attractive in me? Whenever we meet,
you give me such a gracious smile."

What attracted me? It was Jesus hidden in the
depths of her soul, Jesus who makes attractive even
what is most bitter.

I have just mentioned my last resort in escaping
defeat in the battle of life . . . to act like a *deserter*.
It is not very honorable, but it has always proved

successful, and I often used it during my novitiate.

Here is an example which will probably make you smile. You had been ill for some days with bronchitis, and I was rather anxious. One morning, I came softly to your infirmary to put away the keys of the Communion grille, for I was sacristan. I was secretly rejoicing at this chance to see you, but one of the Sisters was afraid I was going to wake you up and in her zeal tried to relieve me of the keys.

I told her very politely that I was just as anxious as she was to make no noise, but that it was my duty to replace them. I know now that it would have been better if I had simply handed them to her, but I did not think so at the time. I tried to push my way in, in spite of her opposition.

Then it happened . . . the noise we were making awakened you, and everything was blamed on me! The Sister made quite a speech, the burden of which was: "It was Sister Thérèse of the Child Jesus who made all the noise."

I simply longed to defend myself, but happily I had a bright idea. I knew I would certainly lose my peace of mind if I tried to justify myself; I knew too that I was not virtuous enough to remain silent in the face of this accusation. There was only one way out—I must run away. No sooner thought than done; I fled! . . . but my heart was beating so violently that I could not go very far, and I sat down on the stairs to enjoy quietly the fruits of my victory.

A strange kind of bravery, but it was better than exposing myself to certain defeat!

When I think back on my days in the novitiate, I

see only too clearly how imperfect I was. I have to laugh at some of the things I did. God is certainly very good to have lifted up my soul and lent it wings. The nets of the hunters can no longer frighten me, for "*a net is set in vain before the eyes of them that have wings.*" (*Prov.* 1:17).

Later on, my present state may appear as most imperfect, but nothing surprises me anymore. And I am not distressed when my helplessness is brought home to me; on the contrary, I make it my boast and expect each day to reveal some imperfection which I had not seen before.

This enlightenment on my nothingness does me more good, in fact, than enlightenment on matters of faith. I remember that "*charity covereth a multitude of sins*" (*Prov.* 10:12) and draw upon the riches opened up by Our Lord in the Gospels. I search the depths of His adorable words and cry with David: "*I have run in the way of Thy commandments when Thou didst enlarge my heart.*" (*Ps.* 118:32).

My heart is opened out by charity alone . . . O Jesus, ever since this heart of mine has been consumed by its gentle flame, I have run with delight in the way of Your *new commandment*, and may I go on doing so until the day when, in Your company of virgins, I will follow You throughout the boundless spaces of eternity, singing Your *new Canticle*, the Canticle of LOVE.

Chapter 10

THE WAY OF LOVE

IN His infinite goodness, Reverend Mother, God has given me the grace to sound the mysterious depths of charity. If I could only tell you all I understand, it would be like the harmonies of Heaven in your ears, but I can only lisp like a little child and would be tempted to ask leave to be silent, if the words of Jesus did not support me.

When the Divine Master says, "*Give to everyone that asketh thee, and of him that taketh away thy goods, ask them not again*" (*Luke* 6:30), I think He means not only the goods of earth, but those of Heaven too. Neither belong to me, in any case, since I renounced the former when I took the vow of poverty, and the latter have only been lent to me by God; He can take them back, and I should have no right to complain about it.

But one's most intimate thoughts, the children of one's heart and mind, are riches which one clings to as one's very own; no one has any right to encroach on them. If, for example, I tell one of the Sisters of some enlightening thought that came to me in meditation, and if she makes it known as if it had come to her, it would seem as though she had taken something that was mine. Or again, if in recreation, someone whispers something amusing to her neighbor and this is repeated out loud without acknowledgement, its author feels as if she has been robbed. She may say nothing at the time, but feels her loss and seizes the first chance she gets to make known, delicately of course, that it was stolen from *her* treasury of thoughts. I could not tell you of such paltry failings, Mother, had I not experienced them myself, and I should have liked to lull myself with the pleasant illusion that they troubled me alone, had you not ordered me to act as spiritual directress to the novices.

This task which you entrusted to me has taught me much, while above all, it makes me practice what I preach. I think it is true to say now that, through grace, I am as detached from the spiritual goods of heart and soul as I am from earthly goods. If any thoughts or words of mine should happen to give pleasure to the Sisters, I am only too glad that they should treat them as their own property. Such thoughts, after all, do not belong to me, but to the Holy Ghost, for has not St. Paul assured us that *"without the Spirit of Love, we cannot even call God Father"*? (Cf. *Rom.* 8:15). I cannot regard such thoughts as my personal property, and so He is very welcome to make use of me to pass them on to others.

Besides, I have been convinced for a long time that, though of course one must not despise anything that helps us to be more closely united to God, such inspirations, however sublime, are worth nothing without deeds.

True, others may profit by these thoughts, so long as they are grateful to God for allowing them to share the banquet of one more privileged, but if it makes the latter self-satisfied, like the Pharisee, she would be like someone dying of hunger at a well-spread table. The guests would take their fill, perhaps even casting envious eyes upon the owner of such riches, while she starved.

Yes, only God can see what is in the bottom of our hearts; we are half-blind. When someone is more enlightened than we are, we conclude that God must love us less. Since when did He lose the right to use anyone He likes to feed His other children with the food they need? He certainly acted in this way in the time of Pharaoh, for He said to him: "*And therefore have I raised thee that I may show My power in thee and My name may be spoken of throughout the earth.*" (*Ex.* 9:16). That was centuries ago, but the Most High has not changed His ways. He has always chosen from among His people those through whom He carries out His work for souls.

Could a canvas painted by an artist think and speak, it certainly would not grumble at being continually touched and retouched by the brush, nor be envious of the brush, knowing that its beauty did not come from the brush, but from the artist who was using it. The brush in turn could take no credit for a masterpiece, just because it was used to paint it, knowing that real artists are never at a loss, rejoice at difficulties, and often for their own amusement use the most wretched and defective instruments.

I am the little brush, Reverend Mother, which Jesus

has chosen to use to paint His likeness on the souls you have entrusted to my care. An artist uses many brushes, or two at least. The first and most important is used to sketch the general background and quickly covers the whole of the canvas, while the second, the smaller one, is used to sketch in detail.

I liken you, Mother, to the more valuable brush which Jesus lovingly takes up when He has in mind some great work upon your children's souls; I am the very little brush He uses afterwards for minor details.

The Divine Artist first took up His little brush on December 8, 1892, and I shall always remember the occasion as one of special grace. I found a companion in the Novitiate when I entered Carmel. She was eight years older than I was, but in spite of this, we became intimate friends and were allowed to talk together about spiritual matters, to develop an affection which showed signs of helping us in the practice of virtue.

I was charmed by her innocence; she was so frank and open, yet her affection for you astonished me, for it was so different from mine, and her conduct seemed to me regrettable in many ways. But God had shown me already that, in His mercy, He never tires of waiting for some people, enlightening them only little by little, so I was careful not to rush things. Reflecting one day that we were allowed to talk, in order, as the Rule says, "to inflame each other with a greater love for our Spouse," I realized sadly that the desired end was not being attained. It was clear that I should have to speak out or else really put an end to conversations which savored too much of the world. I implored Our

Lord to help me to speak gently but convincingly, or rather, to speak through me Himself.

He heard my prayer, for "*those who look upon Him shall be enlightened*" (Cf. *Ps.* 33:6), and "*to the upright a light is risen in the darkness.*" (*Ps.* 111:4). I apply the first text to myself, the second to my companion, whose heart was truly upright.

When we met for our next talk, the poor Sister saw at once from my manner that things were not the same as before. She blushed as she sat down beside me. I put my arms around her and gently spoke my mind, telling her what true love really is, proving that her natural affection for you was only a form of self-love and making known the sacrifices I myself had had to make at the beginning of my spiritual life in this very matter. Soon her tears were mingling with mine. She humbly admitted that I was right and she was wrong, promised to begin a new life and asked me as a favor always to point out her faults.

From then on, our affection for one another became entirely spiritual, and the words of the Holy Spirit were fulfilled in us: "*A brother that is helped by his brother is like a strong city.*" (*Prov.* 18:19).

You know very well, Mother, that I had no intention of turning her away from you, only of making it clear that true love feeds on sacrifice and becomes more pure and strong the more our natural satisfaction is denied.

I remember that as a postulant I was sometimes so violently tempted to seek some crumb of comfort for my own satisfaction that I had to hurry past your cell and cling to the banister to prevent myself from going back. A thousand and one excuses for yielding to my natural inclination presented themselves to me; there were so many things to ask about. I am only too glad, now, that I denied myself from the beginning of my spiritual life, for I enjoy already the reward promised to those who fight with courage. I no longer feel that I must deny my heart all consolation, for it is fixed on God. . . . It has loved Him alone, and this has gradually so developed it that it is able to love those whom He loves with a tenderness incomparably deeper than any selfish, barren affection.

I have already mentioned the first work you and Jesus executed with the little brush; it was only an introduction to the masterpiece to come.

As soon as I entered the sanctuary of souls, I saw at a glance that the task was quite beyond me, and placing myself in the arms of God, I did what a baby would do if it were frightened: I hid my head on my Father's shoulder and said: "You see, O Lord, that I am too little to feed Your children. If You want me to give each one, on Your behalf, just what she needs, then fill my hand, and without leaving Your arms, without so much as turning my head, I will pass on Your riches to those who come to me for food.

"If they like it, then I shall know it is You, not I, to whom they are indebted; but if they grumble because they find it bitter, I will not fret. I will try to convince them that it comes from You and take good care to offer them no choice."

The very fact that, left to myself, I could do nothing, made my task seem all the more simple; there was only one thing for me to do, unite myself more and more to God, knowing that He would give all the rest in addition.

This was no vain hope; no matter how often I have to feed the souls of my Sisters, my hand is always full.

I assure you that had I acted in any other way, had I relied upon my own resources, I should have had to lay down my arms at once.

At first sight, it appears easy to do good to souls, to make them love God more, and mold them according to one's own ideas, but in practice one finds that one can no more do good to souls without God's help than make the sun shine in the night.

One realizes that one must completely forget one's own ideas and tastes, and guide souls along the particular path indicated for them by Jesus, not along one's own. And this is not the worst; what costs me most is having to look out for their faults, their slightest imperfections, and then fight against them to the death.

I was going to say "unhappily for me," but I will not play the coward; I will say "happily for my Sisters" instead, for ever since I put myself in the arms of Jesus, I have been like a sentry watching for the enemy from the highest turret of a castle. I miss nothing and am often amazed that I see things so clearly, while I have every sympathy with Jonas, who fled before the face of the Lord rather than announce the ruin of Nineveh. I would rather be corrected a thousand times than correct anyone else once, yet I am convinced that this is as it should be, for if one does it according to one's natural inclination, the person in the wrong will not recognize it; she will simply say to herself: "The Sister who has to instruct me is annoyed about something and is venting her vexation on me, though I am full of the best intentions."

Here, as in everything else, I must deny myself and make sacrifices. It is the same with a letter; it will be fruitless, I feel, unless I have had to overcome a certain amount of repugnance, and unless it has been written solely under obedience.

Whenever I am talking to one of the novices, I take care to mortify myself by never asking questions out of curiosity. If she begins to talk about something very interesting, then changes the subject to something that does not interest me at all, I never draw her attention to the fact, for I am sure that self-seeking leads to no good.

I know that your lambs think I am very strict, and if they were to read this, they would say that it does not seem to worry me in the least to have to chase after them and tell them when they soil their lovely fleece, or leave some of their wool caught in the wayside briars. But whatever they say, they know in their hearts that I love them, that there is no danger of my imitating the hireling *"who seeth the wolf coming and leaveth the sheep and flieth."* (*John* 10:12). I am ready *"to lay down my life for them"* (*John* 10:15), and I love them with such a pure love that I do not want them to know it. I have never, thanks to God's grace, tried to win their hearts to myself; I know that my task is to lead them to God and to you, Mother, His visible representative here below, to whom they owe respect and love.

In teaching others, as I have said, I have learned

a lot. I saw from the very beginning that everyone has to go through much the same struggle, though from another point of view, there are vast differences between one soul and another; and because they are so different, I can never treat them in the same way.

In some cases I have to make myself very small and not be afraid to humble myself by telling them about my own struggles and failures. It is not so hard for them, then, to make known their own faults, and it makes them happier to know that I have learned all about it from my own experience.

In other cases, the only way is to be firm and never go back on anything; humbling oneself would be regarded as a sign of weakness. I want to do my duty, no matter what the cost, and Our Lord has given me the grace to face everything.

More than once, I have heard someone say: "You will have to treat me gently if you want to get anything out of me; if you treat me with severity, you will get nowhere."

But I know very well that no one is any judge in his own case, and a child naturally makes a fuss under the surgeon's knife, sure that the remedy is worse than the disease; but he will be delighted at being able to run about and play when he finds, a few days later, that he has been cured.

It is just the same with souls: before long, they are quite ready to admit that they would rather have a little bitterness than sugar. Sometimes the change which takes place in a soul from one day to the next seems like magic. "You were quite right to be so short with me yesterday," one told me. "I was very annoyed about it at first, but when I thought about the whole matter afterwards, I saw how right you were. As I left your cell, I thought that this was the end and said to myself: 'I am going to tell our Mother that I will have nothing more to do with Sister Thérèse of the Child Jesus,' but I knew it was the devil who put this thought into my head, and I had an idea that you were praying for me. I grew calm, and light began to dawn. Everything is clear now, so I have come back. I want you to enlighten me."

Then, only too glad to follow the impulse of my heart, I hastened to offer her less bitter food. That was all very well, but I soon saw that I must not go too far; one word too much might undermine the lofty edifice built upon tears. If I were unlucky enough to say anything to mitigate the strictures of the night before, I should find the Sister trying to escape the main issue. When that happens, I take refuge in prayer; I have only to turn to Mary, and Jesus triumphs over everything; indeed, all my strength lies in prayer and sacrifice. They are my invincible arms, and I know from experience that I can conquer hearts with these more surely than I can with words. During Lent, two years ago, a novice came to me all radiant. "You'll never guess what I dreamed last night," she said. "I was with my rather worldly sister, and wanting to win her from all earthly vanities, I explained the following words to her from your hymn, '*To Live by Love*':

> 'Jesus, Thou dost repay a hundredfold
> All that we lose in loving Thee.

Take then, the perfume of my life
Nor give it back to me.

"I felt certain that my words had penetrated her soul to its depths and was overwhelmed with a sense of joy. It seems to me now that God wants me to give Him this soul. What do you think? Should I write to her at Easter, tell her my dream and say that Jesus wants her as His bride?"

I said that at least she could ask permission. Lent was not nearly over, so you were surprised, Mother, at being asked so far in advance, and, obviously inspired by God, you told her that Carmelites should save souls by prayer, rather than by letter. On hearing this decision, I said to her: "We must set to work and pray very hard. What joy if we were answered by the end of Lent!"

How infinitely merciful Our Lord is! At the end of Lent, one more soul gave herself to Jesus. It was a veritable miracle of grace, a miracle obtained by the fervor of a humble novice.

The power of prayer is certainly wonderful. One might liken it to a queen who always has free access to the king and can obtain everything she asks.

It is not necessary to read from a book beautiful prayers composed for our particular need before we can be heard. If this were the case, I should certainly have to be pitied.

The daily recitation of Divine Office is a great joy to me in spite of my unworthiness, but apart from this, I have not the courage to make myself search for wonderful prayers in books; there are so many of them, and it gives me a headache. In any case, each one seems more beautiful than the one before. As I cannot say all of them, and do not know which to choose, I just act like a child who can't read; I tell God, quite simply, all that I want to say, and He always understands.

Prayer, for me, is simply a raising of the heart, a simple glance towards Heaven, an expression of love and gratitude in the midst of trial, as well as in times of joy; in a word, it is something noble and supernatural expanding my soul and uniting it to God.

Whenever my soul is so dry that I am incapable of a single good thought, I always say an *Our Father* or a *Hail Mary* very slowly, and these prayers alone cheer me up and nourish my soul with divine food.

But what has happened to my story? I have lost myself in a maze of thoughts. Do please forgive me for wandering so far from the point. I know my story is nothing but a tangled skein, but it is the best I can do. I simply write things down as they come, fishing at random in the pool of my heart and offering you my catch as I draw it out.

To return to what I was saying about the novices. They often tell me: "You seem to have an answer for everything; I thought you were going to be caught this time. Where do you find it all?" Some of them are simple enough to believe that I can see what is going on in their souls, just because I sometimes anticipate what they are going to say—without any revelation! The senior novice was suffering very much under the weight of a great sorrow, which she was determined to hide from me, and had spent a night of agony trying not to cry because she was afraid her eyes would give her away. She met me calm and smiling, talked just as usual, and if possible, was more friendly than ever. I told her quite simply: "Something is troubling you. I'm sure of it." She looked at me at once in blank amazement and was so taken back that her surprise infected me, giving me an indescribable sense of the supernatural. God was there, very close. Without my knowing, for I do not possess the gift of reading souls, I had spoken as one inspired. It was not hard to set her soul completely at rest after that.

Now I am going to tell you what I have gained most of all in my dealings with the novices. You know they are quite free to say whatever they think, whether it is good or otherwise, and since they do not owe me the respect due to a Novice Mistress, they feel no difficulties here as far as I am concerned.

I cannot say that Jesus makes me walk the path of outward humiliations; He is quite content to humble me in my inmost soul. I am a success as far as everyone else can see, and if one may use such an expression with regard to the religious life, I walk the perilous path of honor, and I understand why my Superiors treat me as they do and why God treats me in the same way.

I would be of little use to you, Mother, if everyone thought I was stupid and incapable of doing anything. That is why our Divine Master has cast a veil over all my shortcomings, exterior or interior. Because of this veil, the novices pay me many compliments which are sincere and therefore not simply flattering, but they do not make me vain because I know what I really am.

I am often worried at receiving nothing but praise, and I grow tired of this food which is over-sweet; then Jesus offers me a tasty salad, seasoned with vinegar and spice. Nothing is left out except the oil, and this makes it more tasty than ever. It is brought to me by the novices when I least expect it. God lifts the veil which hides my imperfections, and my Sisters see me as I am, not much to their liking.

With a delightful frankness, they tell me what a time I give them and what they dislike about me. They could hardly be more candid if talking about someone else because they know that I like them to act like this. Not only does it give me pleasure; it is a delicious feast which fills my soul with joy.

How can anything so naturally repugnant fill me with joy? If I had not experienced it, I could never have believed it possible. One day, when I wanted very much to be humiliated, a young postulant happened to gratify my desire to such an extent that I could not help being reminded of the time when Semei cursed David, and I repeated the latter's words to myself: *"Yea, it is the Lord who hath bidden him say all these things."* (Cf. *2 Kgs.* 16:10).

That is how God looks after me; He cannot always offer me the strengthening bread of humiliation, but now and then He lets me eat *"the crumbs which fall from the table of the children."* (*Mark* 7:28). How merciful He is!

Since even on earth I am trying to sing with you

His infinite mercies, I must tell you of another of the many benefits my small task has brought me.

Up to now, whenever I saw a Sister acting in a way I did not like and which I thought was against the Rule, I used to say to myself: "If only I could warn her about it and tell her where she is wrong"; but now that this is my task, I do not feel at all like that. Whenever I notice anyone who is not a novice doing anything wrong, I heave a sigh of relief. Thank goodness it is not my business to correct her! I hasten to make excuses for her, crediting her with her undoubted good intentions.

All through my illness you have showered attentions on me, and this has taught me a great deal about charity. No remedy seems too expensive to you; if one fails, then you untiringly try another. You take such care of me at recreation: there must be no drafts. All this makes me realize that I should be just as compassionate concerning the spiritual infirmities of my Sisters as you are concerning my physical ones.

I have noticed that the most saintly nuns are the most loved; everyone wants to be with them and to do little things for them without waiting to be asked. And I have noticed lastly that those who do not mind whether they get attention and respect or not, find themselves surrounded by every kind of love. One might apply the words of St. John of the Cross to them: "All good things have been granted me since I no longer seek them out of selfishness." [1]

---

1. These words are found in St. John's symbolic representation of "The Ascent of Mount Carmel."

On the other hand, no one wants to be with those who are imperfect; one treats them as the courtesy of our religious life demands, but one keeps out of their way for fear of saying something unkind.

By imperfections, I do not mean merely spiritual imperfections; none of us will be perfect this side of Heaven in any case! I include the lack of common sense and up-bringing and the over-sensitiveness of certain people, which makes life so unpleasant for everyone else. I know perfectly well that such defects are so deeply rooted as to be beyond all hope of cure, but I am just as sure you would never cease taking care of me and doing all you could for me, even though I went on being ill for years.

What do I conclude from this? That I must seek out the company of the Sisters who, naturally speaking, repel me, and be their Good Samaritan. Often a single word, a friendly smile, is enough to give a depressed or lonely soul fresh life.

Nevertheless, I do not always want to practice charity merely to bring consolation. I would soon be discouraged if that were so, for something said with the best of intentions may be taken completely the wrong way; so, in order not to waste my time and trouble, I try to do everything to give pleasure to Our Lord and to follow out this Gospel precept: "*When thou makest a supper, call not thy friends nor thy brethren, lest perhaps they also invite thee again and a recompense be made to thee. But when thou makest a feast, call the poor, the maimed, the blind and the lame, and thou shalt be blessed, because they have naught to make thee recompense.*" (*Luke* 14:12-14).

"*And thy Father, who seeth in secret, will repay thee.*" (*Matt.* 6:4).

A spiritual feast of gentle, joyful love is all I can set before my Sisters; I do not know of any other and want to follow the example of St. Paul, rejoicing with all who rejoice. I know he wept with those who weep, and my feasts are not always without their share of tears, but I always try to turn them into smiles, for "*the Lord loveth the cheerful giver.*" (*2 Cor.* 9:7).

I remember one act of charity inspired by God when I was still a novice. It did not seem much, but our Heavenly Father, "*who seeth in secret,*" has rewarded me already in this life without my having to wait for the next. It was before Sister St. Peter became a complete invalid. At ten to six every evening, someone had to go out from meditation to take her along to the refectory. It cost me a lot to offer my services because I knew how difficult she was to please, almost impossible, but it was a wonderful chance, and I did not want to miss it. I remembered the words of Our Lord: "*As long as you did it to one of these My brethren, you did it to Me.*" (*Matt.* 25:40).

So, very humbly I offered to help her, and after a lot of trouble, she was prevailed upon to accept me. I set about my task with so much good will that in the end I succeeded completely. Every evening, when I saw her shaking her hourglass about, I knew that she meant: "Let us go." Summoning up all my courage, I got up, and then a real ceremony began. Her stool had to be moved; it must be carried *just so*; one must not go too quickly. At last we set off.

I had to go behind her and support her by her

belt, and I used to do this as gently as I possibly could; but if by some mischance she chanced to stumble, she thought I was not holding her properly, she was going to fall over: "My goodness! you are going much too fast. I shall hurt myself." I try to go more slowly: "Why don't you keep up with me? I don't feel your hand. You are letting me go. I shall fall over! How right I was when I said you were much too young to look after me!"

At last we arrived at the refectory without any more mishaps. Then there was more trouble! She had to be manœuvred into her place very skillfully so as not to be hurt in any way; her sleeves must be rolled back, again *just so*; then I could go.

It was not long before I noticed that she could not cut her bread very easily, so I used to do that too before finally leaving her. As she had never told me she wanted me to do it, she was touched, and it was this unlooked-for act of kindness which won her heart completely; though I learned later that what touched her most of all was the fact that when I had done all I could, I always gave her, so she said, my "very best smile."

That was all a long time ago, Mother, yet Our Lord allows the memory to linger in all its fragrance, like a breath from Heaven.

I was carrying out my usual task one winter evening; it was cold and dark. Suddenly, far away, from some distant orchestra, there came the sound of music. I seemed to see a richly furnished room, all bright with lights and resplendent, where young ladies, beautifully dressed, exchanged the countless courtesies of society life. My eyes turned back to the poor invalid I was helping. In place of the music, plaintive groans from time to time; in place of the resplendent room, nothing but the cloister walls, austere, scarcely visible in the flickering light. The contrast softly touched my soul. Our Lord poured in the light of truth, which shines far brighter than the shadowy light of earthly pleasures. I would not exchange the ten minutes spent upon my act of charity for a thousand years of such worldly delights.

If to remember in the time of suffering on the battlefield that God has withdrawn us from the world can be such sweet delight, what will it be on high, when, in everlasting glory and eternal rest, we realize what a grace it was to be picked out to dwell in His home on earth in the very outer court of Heaven.

My practice of charity is not always accompanied by such exhilaration, but at the beginning of my religious life, Jesus wanted me to understand how sweet it is to see Him in the souls of His spouses; so I escorted Sister St. Peter with so much love that I could not possibly have done it better had it been Our Lord Himself. Nor have I found the practice of charity always so easy, as you will soon see. I will tell you a few of my many struggles, to prove it.

For a long time I had to kneel during meditation near a Sister who could not stop fidgeting; if it was not with her Rosary, it was with goodness knows what else. Maybe no one else noticed it; I have a very sensitive ear. But you have no idea how much it annoyed me. I wanted to turn around and glare at the culprit to make her be quiet, but deep in my heart I felt that the best thing to do was to put up with it patiently, for the love of God first of all, and also not to hurt her feelings. So I kept quiet, bathed in perspiration often enough, while my prayer was nothing more than the prayer of suffering! In the end, I tried to find some way of bearing it peacefully and joyfully, at least in my inmost heart; then I even tried to like this wretched little noise.

It was impossible not to hear it, so I turned my whole attention to listening really closely to it, as if it were a magnificent concert, and spent the rest of the time offering it to Jesus. It was certainly not the prayer of quiet!

Another time, washing handkerchiefs in the laundry opposite a Sister who kept on splashing me with dirty water, I was tempted to step back and wipe my face to show her that I would be obliged if she would be more careful. But why be foolish enough to refuse treasures offered so generously? I took care to hide my exasperation.

I tried hard to enjoy being splashed with dirty water, and by the end of half an hour, I had acquired a real taste for this novel form of aspersion. How fortunate to find this spot where such treasures were being given away! I would come back as often as I could.

So you see, Mother, what a *very little* soul I am! I can only offer *very little* things to God. These little sacrifices bring great peace of soul, but I often let the chance of making them slip by. However, it does not discourage me. I put up with having a little less peace, and try to be more careful the next time.

Our Lord makes me so happy! It is so easy and

delightful to serve Him here below. Again, I must confess, He has always given me what I wanted, or rather, made me want what He desires to give.

Just before my dreadful temptations against faith, I said to myself: "I certainly do not suffer from any great exterior trials, and God will have to lead me by some other path than at present if I am going to have inward ones. I do not think He will do that, yet this peace cannot go on forever. I wonder what He will do about it."

The answer was not long in coming. I discovered that He whom I love is never at a loss. Without changing my path, He sent me this great trial, and all my joys were tinged with a wholesome bitterness.

It is not only when He has a trial in store that He stirs up my desire for what is to come. I had cherished for a long time the desire to have a brother who was a priest, but I thought it was quite impossible. I often thought that if my young brothers had not flown off to Heaven, I might have been happy enough to see one of them at the altar. It was a great disappointment. Yet see how God has more than fulfilled my dream!

All I had wanted was one brother to remember me at the altar every day, but He has spiritually united me to *two* of His Apostles.

I must tell you, Mother, exactly how our Divine Master granted my desires.

Our holy mother, St. Teresa, sent me my first brother on my feast day in 1895. It was washing day, and I was hard at work when Mother Agnes of Jesus, Prioress at the time, took me aside and read to me the letter of a young seminarian. St. Teresa had inspired him, so he said, to ask for a Sister who would devote herself especially to his salvation and to the salvation of those souls he was soon to look after. He promised that he would always remember his new Sister in his Mass.

It was I who was chosen to become the Sister of this future missionary, and I cannot tell you, Mother, what a joy this was to me! It was such an unexpected answer that I felt as happy as a child. I say that because I cannot remember ever having been so happy since my childhood, when my heart seemed all too small to contain its vivid joys.

I had not, I say, felt as happy as this for years; it was as though my heart were born again, as if forgotten chords of music had been touched for the first time.

Realizing my new obligations, I set to work with redoubled fervor, and from time to time wrote letters to my new brother.

Doubtless, missionaries are best helped by prayer and sacrifice, yet sometimes when Jesus wills to unite two souls for His greater glory, He lets them exchange their ideas so that they may encourage one another to love God more and more. However, this must be done only at the express request of one's Superiors; if one *asked* to be allowed to write, it would do more harm than good, if not to the missionary at least to the Carmelite, whose way of life obliges her to be continually retired within herself. Such correspondence, however infrequent, instead of uniting her to God, would occupy her mind too much and achieve nothing. She would probably imagine that she was working wonders, when in fact, under the guise of zeal, she had done no more than take on a useless distraction.

Yet what is all this but an equally unnecessary dissertation, even though it may not be a distraction? I shall never cure myself of these digressions; you must be quite tired of them. Do forgive me, though at the first opportunity, I shall be just as bad again.

Last year, at the end of May, it was your turn to give me a brother, my second one. I pointed out that I was already offering what little merits I had for one future apostle and could not possibly make them spin out for two, but you told me that obedience would give them twice the value. At the bottom of my heart, I felt sure that this was true. The zeal of a Carmelite should embrace the whole world, so I even hoped, with the grace of God, to be of service to more than two missionaries. I pray for all, including priests in our own country whose work is often just as hard as that of the missionaries among the pagans.

In fact, like our Mother St. Teresa, I want to be "a daughter of the Church" and pray for all the intentions of the Vicar of Christ. This is my one great aim. Had my brothers lived, I should have joined in their good works without neglecting the worldwide interests of the Church, and in the same way I can share those of the new brothers given me by Jesus.

All that I have belongs to each of them; God is far too good and too generous to divide it. He is so rich that He gives unstintingly all that I ask, even without my having to spend time in making up long lists of requests.

Though I have only these two brothers, and my Sisters the novices, my days are not long enough to detail all their needs, and I would probably forget something really important. Complicated methods are not for simple souls like me, so Our Lord Himself has inspired me with a very simple way of fulfilling my obligations.

One day after Communion, He taught me the meaning of the following words in the *Canticle of Canticles*: "*Draw me . . . we will run after Thee to the odor of Thy ointments.*" (*Cant.* 1:3).

It is therefore unnecessary, my Jesus, to say "draw those I love in drawing me." It is quite enough to say simply, "*Draw me.*" For once a soul has been captivated by the odor of Your ointments, she cannot run alone; by the very fact of being drawn to You herself, she draws all the souls she loves after her. Just as a mighty river carries with it all it meets into the ocean's depths, so, my Jesus, a soul which plunges into the boundless ocean of Your love bears all her treasures with her. You know what my treasures are; they are the souls You made one with mine, treasures which You Yourself have given me, so that I even dare to make my own the very words You used on the last evening You spent as a mortal traveler on earth. I do not know, my Jesus, when my exile will come to an end. Many an evening yet may find me singing Your mercies here below, but sometime my last evening too will come, and then I want to be able to say:

"*I have glorified Thee upon earth; I have finished the work which Thou gavest me to do. I have mani-*

*fested Thy name to the men whom Thou hast given me
out of the world. Thine they were, and to me Thou
gavest them; and they have kept Thy word. Now they
have known that all things which Thou hast given me
are from Thee, because the words which Thou gavest
me I have given to them; and they have received them,
and have known for certain that I came forth from
Thee. And they have believed that Thou didst send me.
I pray for them. I pray not for the world, but for them
whom Thou hast given me, because they are Thine. And
all mine are Thine, and Thine are mine, and I am glorified in them. And now I am no more in the world,
and these are in the world, and I come to Thee.*

*"Holy Father, keep them in Thy name, whom Thou
hast given me, that they may be one as we also are one.
And now I come to Thee, and these things I speak in
the world, that they may have my joy filled in themselves. I do not ask that Thou take them away out of
the world, but that Thou preserve them from evil. They
are not of the world, as I am not of the world. And
not for them only do I pray, but for those also who
through their word shall believe in me.*

*"Father, I will that where I am, they also whom Thou
hast given me may be with me, that they may see my
glory which Thou hast given me, because Thou hast loved
me before the foundation of the world. And I have made
known Thy Name unto them, and will make it known,
that the love wherewith Thou hast loved me may be in
them and I in them." (John* 17:4-26).

O Jesus, I long to repeat these words of Yours before
I surrender myself into Your arms. Perhaps I am being
rather too bold? I do not think so. I have treated

You in this way for a long time, and You have not minded. You have said to me, as the prodigal son's father said to his elder son, "All that is Mine is thine," so Your words are mine too, and I can use them to draw down our Heavenly Father's favors on the souls entrusted to my care.

You know, my God, that my one desire has ever been to love You alone; Your glory has been my one ambition. Your love has gone before me from the days of my childhood; it has grown with me, and now it is an abyss so deep that I cannot sound it.

Love calls to love, and mine longs to fill the abyss of Yours in its flight to You, but it is not even a drop of dew lost in that sea. If I am to love You as You love me, I must borrow Your love; I can find peace no other way.

It seems to me, my Jesus, that You could never have lavished on anyone more love than You have lavished on me, and that is why I do not fear to ask You to love those You have given me . . . *even as You have loved me.* (Cf. *John* 17:23).

If one day in Heaven I should find that You love them more than me, I shall be only too glad, recognizing that they must have merited more on earth, but at the moment, I cannot conceive how anyone could have a greater love than the love You have granted me, without any merit on my part.

I never meant to write as I have just done, Mother; I am quite astounded! When I was quoting from the Gospels, "*The words which Thou gavest me I have given unto them,*" I was thinking of the novices, not of my brothers; I do not set myself up to teach missionaries! To them I applied the passage from the prayer of Our Lord: "*I do not ask that Thou shouldst take them out of the world. . . . I pray also for them who through their word shall believe in Thee.*" (*John* 17:15, 20).

I could not possibly forget the souls they are going to win by their preaching and their sufferings.

But I have not told you yet all that this passage from the *Canticle of Canticles* means to me: "*Draw me . . . we will run. . . .*" (*Cant.* 1:3).

"*No man,*" says Our Lord, "*can come to Me, except the Father, who has sent Me, draw him*" (*John* 6:44); and later He teaches us that we have only to knock and it will be opened to us; to seek and we shall find; to hold out our hands humbly, and they will be filled; adding that, "*if you ask the Father anything in My name, He will give it to you.*" (*John* 16:23).

I am sure that is why the Holy Spirit, long before Jesus was born, inspired this prophetic prayer, "*Draw me, we will run.*"

In asking to be drawn, we are seeking to be closely united to the captivating object of our love.

If fire and iron were endowed with reason, and the iron were to say "*Draw me,*" surely this would prove that it wanted to be so identified with the fire as to share its very substance. This is just what I ask. I want Jesus so to draw me into the flames of His love, so to make me one with Himself that He may live and act in me. I feel that the more the fire of love inflames my heart, the more I shall say, "*Draw me,*" and the more swiftly those who are around about me will run "*in the sweet odor of the Beloved.*"

We will run, indeed, all of us, for souls on fire with love cannot remain inactive. Like Mary, they may sit at the feet of Jesus, listening while His gentle words inflame their love, giving Him nothing, so it seems, and yet really giving Him more than a Martha who is anxious about "*many things.*" (*Luke* 10:41). Not that Jesus condemns the work she is doing, only the fuss she makes about it; after all, His own Mother humbly performed those very same tasks when she used to prepare meals for the Holy Family.

It is a lesson which all the Saints have understood, particularly those who have spread the light of the Faith throughout the world. St. Paul, St. Augustine, St. Thomas Aquinas, St. John of the Cross, St. Teresa and so many other friends of God; surely it was in prayer that they acquired that wonderful knowledge which captivates even the greatest of minds?

"Give me a fulcrum," said Archimedes, "and with a lever I will move the world." He was asking the impossible, and yet this is just what the Saints have been given. Their fulcrum is none other than Almighty God Himself; their lever, prayer, the prayer which enkindles the fire of love. It is with this lever that they have uplifted the world, and with this lever those who are still fighting in the world will go on raising it until the End of Time.

All that remains for me to tell you now is what *the sweet odor of the Beloved* means to me. Since Jesus has gone to Heaven now, I can only follow the traces He has left behind. But how bright these traces are! How fragrant and divine! I have only to glance at the Gospels; at once this fragrance from the life of

Jesus reaches me, and I know which way to run: to the lowest, not the highest place! Leaving the Pharisee to push himself forward, I pray humbly like the Publican, but full of confidence.

Yet most of all, I follow the example of Mary Magdalene, my heart captivated by her astonishing, or rather loving audacity, which so won the heart of Jesus. It is not because I have been preserved from mortal sin that I fly to Jesus with such confidence and love; even if I had all the crimes possible on my conscience, I am sure I should lose none of my confidence. Heartbroken with repentance, I would simply throw myself into my Saviour's arms, for I know how much He loves the Prodigal Son. I have heard what He said to Mary Magdalene, to the woman taken in adultery, and to the Samaritan woman. No one can make me frightened any more, because I know what to believe about His mercy and His love; I know that, in the twinkling of an eye, all those thousands of sins would be consumed as a drop of water cast into a blazing fire.

In the lives of the Desert Fathers we are told that one of them converted a public sinner whose doings had scandalized the whole countryside. Touched by grace, she set out into the desert after the Saint to do rigorous penance, but on the first night of her journey, before she had even reached her retreat, her loving sorrow was so great that it severed all ties with earth, and the hermit saw her soul, that very moment, carried by the Angels up into the arms of God.

It is a striking illustration of what I want to say, but one cannot put these things into words.

Chapter 11

IMMENSE DESIRES

M^Y darling Sister, you have asked me to leave
you something, and as our Mother has given
me permission, I am delighted to come and pour out
my heart to one who is doubly a sister to me, to one
who lent me her voice when I could not speak for
myself, to promise I would never serve anyone but
Jesus.

Dearest Godmother, it is the little child you offered
to Our Lord who is speaking to you tonight, the little child who loves you as much as a child loves its
mother. You will never know the overflowing gratitude that fills my heart until we get to Heaven.

You want to know what secrets Jesus has entrusted
to your little child, and yet He has entrusted them
to you as well, I know, because who but you taught
me to listen to His voice?

All the same, I will try to write a few lines, in spite
of the fact that I feel it is quite impossible to put
into words things the heart itself can scarcely grasp.

You probably imagine that my life is one long consolation; if only you knew! My only consolation lies
in not having any here below.

191

Jesus instructs me in secret, never showing Himself, never letting me hear His voice. He does not even make use of books, because I do not understand what I read. However, now and then a phrase brings me consolation, like the following one which came to me at the end of a meditation spent in dryness: "Here is the master I give you to teach you all you have to do. I want you to study the Book of Life, which contains the *science of love*."[1]

The science of love! A phrase which echoes softly in my soul. I desire no other science, and like the Spouse in the *Canticle of Canticles*, "*having given up all the substance of my house for love, I reckon it as nothing.*" (*Cant.* 8:7).

I know it; love alone can make us pleasing to God, so I desire no other treasure.

Jesus has chosen to show me the only way which leads to the Divine Furnace of love; it is the way of childlike self-surrender, the way of a child who sleeps, afraid of nothing, in its father's arms.

"*Whosoever is a little one, let him come unto Me*" (*Prov.* 9:4), says the Holy Spirit through the lips of Solomon, and the same Spirit of Love tells us also that "*to him that is little, mercy is granted.*" (*Wis.* 6:7).

In His name, the prophet Isaias has revealed that on the Last Day "*the Lord shall feed His flock like a shepherd; He shall gather together the lambs with His arm, and shall take them up into His bosom.*" (*Is.* 40:11). As if all this were not proof enough, the same prophet, piercing the depths of eternity with eyes

---

1. Words spoken by Our Lord to St. Margaret Mary.

inspired, cried out in the name of Our Lord: "*You shall be carried at the breasts, and upon the knees they shall caress you. As one whom the mother caresseth, so will I comfort you.*" (*Is.* 66:12, 13).

My darling Sister, one can only remain silent, one can only weep for gratitude and love, after words like these. If only everyone weak and imperfect like me felt as I do, no one would despair of reaching the heights of love, for Jesus does not ask for glorious deeds. He asks only for self-surrender and for gratitude.

"*I will not take,*" He says, "*the he-goats from out of thy flocks, for all the beasts of the forest are mine, the cattle on the hill and the oxen. I know all the fowls of the air. If I were hungry I would not tell thee, for the world is mine, and the fullness thereof. Shall I eat the flesh of bullocks, or shall I drink the blood of goats? OFFER TO GOD THE SACRIFICE OF PRAISE AND THANKSGIVING.*" (*Ps.* 49:9-14). Jesus claims no more from us; He does not need our works, only our *LOVE*.

Yet He who declares that He need not tell us if He is hungry, does not hesitate to *beg* the Samaritan woman for a *drop of water*. He was thirsty! But when He said, "*Give Me to drink*" (*John* 4:7), it was this unhappy woman's love that the Creator of the Universe was seeking; He thirsted for love, and He is more thirsty than ever now. Indifference and ingratitude are all He finds among the world's disciples; even among His own, He finds so few surrendering themselves without reserve to the tenderness of His infinite love.

How fortunate we are to understand the intimate secrets of our Spouse! If you, my darling Sister, were to write down all you know of this, what wonderful reading it would make!

But I know you would rather keep the "*secrets of the King*" (*Tob.* 12:7) locked up in the bottom of your heart, though to me you say that "*it is honourable to reveal the works of God.*" (*Tob.* 12:7). Your silence is the better part, I think, for it is quite impossible to put heavenly secrets into earthly words.

Page after page I could write and still find I had scarcely begun. There are so many ways of looking at things, and so many infinitely varied shades, that the palette of the Divine Painter alone can provide me, when the darkness of this life has passed, with the heavenly colors capable of bringing out the loveliness discovered to my soul.

Nevertheless, since you have told me you long to understand as far as possible my heart's deepest feelings, since you want me to set down the most consoling dream I have ever had, and my "little doctrine," as you call it, I will write the following pages for you. I think it would be easier if I say what I have to say as though to Our Lord. You will perhaps think it sounds rather exaggerated, but I assure you really and truly that there is no exaggeration in my heart. There, all is calm and peace.

O Jesus, the tender way You lead my soul is beyond all telling. From Easter, the radiant feast of Your triumph, until May, a storm was raging in its depths, but then the dark night was lit by the pure rays of the light of Your grace. I thought of the mysterious dreams You sometimes give to those You love and told myself that such consolations were not for me; night was my lot, always darkest night. Amid the storm I fell asleep.

The very next day—it was May 10th—just as the dawn was breaking, though before I was awake, I found myself walking in a gallery with our Mother. Without knowing how they got there, I suddenly saw three Carmelites in their mantles and long veils. I knew they had come from Heaven. Then I thought: "If only I could see the face of one of these Carmelites! I would be so happy!"

As if she had heard me, the tallest of these Saints advanced toward me. I fell on my knees, and then to my joy she raised her veil, or rather, cast it all about me. I recognized her at once; it was the Venerable Mother Anne of Jesus, the Foundress of Carmel in France.

How lovely she was; there was an unearthly beauty about her face, and though the heavy veil enveloped us, it seemed transfused with a gentle light I cannot describe. It seemed to be shining from within, but it did not cast any rays.

She kissed me tenderly, and when I saw how much she loved me, I took courage and spoke to her: "Tell me, Mother, I beg of you, is God going to leave me here much longer? Will He come and fetch me soon?"

She smiled most tenderly, and said: "Soon . . . yes, soon . . . I promise you."

"Answer me something more, Mother; does God want anything more from me than the little things I do for Him, and my desires? Is He pleased with me?"

A new light seemed to suffuse her face at once, and her expression appeared to me incomparably more tender.

"God asks no more of you," she said, ". . . and He is pleased with you; very, very pleased."

She took my head between her hands, and I cannot possibly express how tender were the kisses that she showered on me. Gladness filled my heart, and remembering my Sisters, I was about to ask for favors for them too, but I awoke.

I cannot say how lighthearted I was! Several months have gone by since this wonderful dream, yet the heavenly charm of it has lost none of its freshness. I can still see her loving gaze, her loving smile; I still seem to feel the touch of all her kisses.

O Jesus, "*Thou didst command the wind and the storm, and there came a great calm.*" (Cf. *Matt.* 8:26).

On waking, I not only believed that Heaven existed, I knew it; and I knew too that it was full of souls who loved me as their own child. The impression of it all remains in my heart, made all the more dear by the fact that until then I had been, I will not say indifferent to the Venerable Mother Anne of Jesus, but forgetful of her unless she happened to be mentioned, which was not very often, and I had never invoked her aid.

Yet now I know and realize that at any rate she had never forgotten me; and this not only makes me love her all the more, but also increases my love for all the Blessed in Heaven.

This grace, my Beloved, was only the prelude to the even greater graces which You willed to lavish on me; let me remind You of them now, and forgive me if it is foolish to want to tell You once again about my hopes and desires, which border on the infinite; yes, forgive me and heal my soul by fulfilling all of them.

To be Your Spouse, my Jesus; to be a Carmelite; to be, through my union with You, a mother of souls, surely this should be enough? Yet I feel the call of more vocations still; I want to be a warrior, a priest, an apostle, a doctor of the Church, a martyr—there is no heroic deed I do not wish to perform. I feel as daring as a crusader, ready to die for the Church upon the battlefield.

If only I were a priest! How lovingly I would bear You in my hands, my Jesus, when my voice had brought You down from Heaven. How lovingly I would give You to souls! Yet while wanting to be a priest, I admire St. Francis of Assisi and envy his humility, longing to imitate him in refusing this sublime dignity.

Such contradictions! How can they be reconciled? I long to bring light to souls, like the prophets and doctors; to go to the ends of the earth to preach Your name, to plant Your glorious Cross, my Beloved, on pagan shores.

One mission field alone would never be enough; all the world, even its remotest islands, must be my mission field. Nor would my mission last a few short years, but from the beginning of the world to the End of Time.

But to be a martyr is what I long for most of all. Martyrdom! I dreamed of it when I was young, and the dream has grown up with me in my little cell in Carmel. I am just as foolish about this because I do not desire any one kind of torture; I would be satisfied only with them all.

I want to be scourged and crucified like You, my Spouse; flayed alive like St. Bartholomew; thrown into boiling oil like St. John; and ground by the teeth of wild beasts like St. Ignatius of Antioch, so that I might become bread worthy of God.

Like St. Agnes and St. Cecilia, I want to offer my neck to the executioner's sword, and like Joan of Arc, murmur the name of Jesus at the burning stake.

My heart thrills at the thought of the undreamed-of torments which will be the lot of Christians in the time of Anti-Christ! I want them all to be my lot!

Open the Book of Life, my Jesus; see all the deeds recorded of the Saints! All these I want to perform for You!

What can You say in the face of all this foolishness of mine, for surely I am the littlest and the weakest soul on earth?

Yet just because I am so weak, You have been pleased to grant my childish little desires, and now You will grant the rest, other desires far greater than the Universe.

These desires became a real martyrdom to me, and so one day, hoping to find alleviation, I opened the Epistles of St. Paul. My eyes lighted on Chapters XII and XIII of his First Epistle to the Corinthians, where he says we cannot all be apostles, prophets and doctors, that the Church is made up of a number of different members, and that the eye cannot also be the hand. The answer was clear enough, but it did not satisfy my desires nor bring me any peace.

"Descending to the depths of my own nothingness, I was then so raised up that I attained my goal."[2] For without being discouraged, I went on reading, and found relief in the following advice: "*Be zealous for the better gifts. And I show unto you a yet more excellent way.*" (*1 Cor.* 12:31). The Apostle goes on to explain that the most perfect gifts are worth nothing without love, and this more excellent way of going to God is Charity.

At last I was at rest! As I thought about the Church's Mystical Body, I could not see myself in any of the members mentioned by St. Paul, or rather, I wanted to see myself in all of them.

Charity gave me the key to *my vocation*. I saw that if the Church was a body made up of different members, the most essential and important one of all would not be lacking; I saw that the Church must have *a heart*, that this heart must be on fire with love. I saw that it was love alone which moved her other members, and that were this love to fail, apostles would no longer spread the Gospel, and martyrs would refuse to shed their blood. I saw that all vocations are summed up in love and that love is all in all, embracing every time and place because it is eternal.

In a transport of ecstatic joy I cried: "Jesus, my Love, I have at last found my vocation; *it is love*! I have found my place in the Church's heart, the place You Yourself have given me, my God. Yes, there in

---

2. From a poem by St. John of the Cross.

the heart of Mother Church *I will be love*; so shall I be all things, so shall my dreams come true."

I have used the expression "ecstatic joy," but this is not quite correct, for it is above all peace which is now my lot; the calm security of the sailor in sight of the beacon guiding him to port. Ah! Love, my radiant beacon light, I know the way to reach You now, and I have found the hidden secret of making all Your flames my own!

I know I am no more than a helpless little child, yet, my Jesus, it is my very helplessness which makes me dare to offer myself as a victim to Your love!

In bygone days, only pure and spotless victims were acceptable to Almighty God; to satisfy Divine Justice, they must be perfect. But now the law of fear is superseded by the law of love, and love has chosen me as a victim, frail and imperfect as I am. It is surely a worthy choice for love to make, since to be wholly satisfied, it must stoop down to nothingness and turn that nothingness to fire.

I know, my God, that "Love is repaid by love alone,"[3] and so I have sought and found a way to ease my heart by giving love for love.

"*Use the riches that make men unjust to find yourselves friends who may receive you into everlasting dwellings.*" (Cf. *Luke* 16:9). You gave this advice to Your disciples, Lord, after You had told them that "*the children of this world are wiser in their generation than the children of light.*" (*Luke* 16:8).

---

3. St. John of the Cross, *Spiritual Canticle*, Commentary on Strophe IX.

A child of light myself, I understood that my desire
to be all things, and my desire to embrace all vocations, were riches which might well make me unjust,
so I made use of them to make friends for myself.

I called to mind the prayer of Eliseus, asking the
prophet Elias for a double portion of his spirit, and
putting myself in the presence of all the Angels and
Saints, I said to them: "I know I am the least of all;
I know how worthless I am; but I also know how
much noble, generous hearts love doing good; so I
beg of all you happy citizens of Heaven to adopt me
as your child. The glory which you help me to acquire
will all redound to you. Hear me and obtain for me,
I beg, a double portion of your love."

I dare not fathom, Lord, all the implications of
my prayer, lest I should find myself crushed beneath
the weight of my audacity!

I take refuge in my title, "a little child." Little children never realize all that their words imply, but if
their father or mother were to come to the throne
and inherit great riches, loving their little ones more
than they love themselves, they would not hesitate to
give them everything they want. They would be foolishly lavish, just to please them, and go even as far
as weakness. Well, I am a child of Holy Church, and
the Church is a Queen, because she is espoused to
You, the King of Kings.

My heart does not yearn for riches or for glory,
not even the glory of Heaven; that belongs by rights
to my brothers, the Angels and Saints. Mine will be
the reflection of that glory which shines upon my
Mother's brow.

No! what I ask for is *love*. Only one thing, my Jesus, to *love You*.

Striking deeds are forbidden me. I cannot preach the Gospel; I cannot shed my blood, but what matter? My brothers do it for me, while I, *a little child*, stay close beside the royal throne and *love* for those who are fighting.

Love proves itself by deeds, and how shall I prove mine? *The little child will scatter flowers* whose fragrant perfume will surround the royal throne, and in a voice that is silver-toned, she will sing the *canticle of love*.

So, my Beloved, shall my short life be spent in Your sight. I can prove my love only by scattering flowers, that is to say, by never letting slip a single little sacrifice, a single glance, a single word; by making profit of the very smallest actions, by doing them all for love.

I want to suffer and even rejoice for love, for this is my way of scattering flowers. Never a flower shall I find but its petals shall be scattered for you; and all the while I will sing, yes, always sing, even when gathering my roses in the midst of thorns; and the longer and sharper the thorns may be, the sweeter shall be my song!

But what use to You, my Jesus, will my songs and flowers be? This fragrant shower, these fragile petals, worthless in themselves, these songs of love from so small a heart will charm You all the same. Yes, I am sure of it; sure that these nothings will give You pleasure. The Church Triumphant will smile on them, and wishing to play with her little one, she will gather up the scattered roses and place them in Your divine hands.

This will invest them with an infinite value, and she will scatter them upon the Church Suffering to put out the flames, and on the Church Militant, to make her victorious.

I love You, Jesus! I love Mother Church, and I never forget that "the least act of pure love is of more value to her than all other works put together."[4]

But is there really pure love in my heart? Perhaps my vast desires are only a dream and nothing but folly? If this is so, I beg You to make it clear to me, because You know I seek the truth. If my desires are overly bold, then take them away, because they are my greatest martyrdom.

And yet, if it should happen that I never reach the heights to which my soul aspires, I swear I shall have tasted far more sweetness in my folly and my martyrdom than I will taste in the midst of eternal joys, unless You work a miracle and take from me the memory of my earthly hopes.

O Jesus, Jesus, if the desire of love brings such delight, what must it be really to possess it and enjoy it for eternity! Yet how can any soul as imperfect as mine aspire to the fullness of Love? How solve this mystery?

My only Friend, why not reserve such boundless aspirations to great souls, souls like eagles, who can wing their way to the stars? I am no eagle, only a

---

4. St. John of the Cross, *Spiritual Canticle*, Commentary on Strophe XXIX.

little fledgling which has not yet lost its down; yet the eagle's heart is mine, and the eagle's eye; and despite my utter littleness, I dare to gaze upon the Sun of Love, burning to take my flight to Him. I long to fly and imitate the eagles, but all I can do is flutter my small wings. I am not strong enough to fly.

What will become of me? Must I die of sorrow at finding myself so helpless? Never! It will not trouble me in the very least. Surrendering myself with daring confidence, I shall simply stay gazing at my Sun until I* die. Nothing will frighten me, neither wind nor rain, and should the Star of Love be blotted out by heavy clouds so that nothing but the night of this life seems to exist, then will be the time for *perfect joy*, the moment to push my confidence to the furthest bounds; I shall take good care to stay just where I am, quite certain that beyond the somber clouds my beloved Sun is shining still!

Even to that extent do I understand Your love for me, my God, and yet, as You know, I very often turn aside from my one task, stray from Your side, and get my half-formed wings drenched in the miserable puddles which I find on earth.

"*I cry like a young swallow*" (*Is.* 38:14) then, a cry which tells You everything, and You remember in Your infinite mercy that *Thou didst not come to call the just, but sinners.* (*Matt.* 9:13).

Should You be deaf to the plaintive twittering of Your wretched creature, should You remain still veiled, I would be content to stay all wet and stiff with cold; I would be glad to suffer just what I had deserved.

I am so happy, my dear Star, to feel little and frail in Your presence, and my heart remains at peace. I know that all the eagles in Your heavenly court look compassionately down on me, protecting and defending me, putting to flight the demon vultures who seek to prey on me.

So I am not at all afraid of them; I am not destined to be their prey, but that of the Divine Eagle.

You, my Savior, You are the Eagle whom I love; and it is You, the Eternal Word, who draw me on; You who flew down to this land of exile, to suffer and die, that You might bear all souls away and plunge them deep into the bosom of the Blessed Trinity, the eternal home of Love.

It is You who, though ascending to inaccessible light, yet stay in our valley of tears, hidden under the appearance of a small white host, to nourish me with Your own substance.

O Jesus, let me tell You that Your love goes as far as folly! In the face of such folly, what can You expect, save that my heart should fly out to You? How can my confidence know any bounds? I know that the Saints have done foolish things, as well as wonderful ones, and my foolishness lies in hoping that Your love accepts me as a victim; it lies in counting on the Angels and Saints to help me, my beloved Eagle, to fly to You on Your own wings!

For as long as You wish, I will stay with my eyes fixed on You, longing to be fascinated by Your divine gaze, longing to be the prey of Your love. I hope that one day You will swoop upon me and carry me off to the furnace of love and plunge me into its glowing abyss, that I may become forever its happy holocaust.

If only, my Jesus, I could tell all *little souls* about Your ineffable condescension!

I feel that if, supposing the impossible, You could find a soul weaker than mine, You would delight in lavishing upon it far more graces still, so long as it abandoned itself with boundless confidence to Your infinite mercy.

But why this desire to tell others the secrets of Your love? Can You not, Yourself, reveal to others what You have revealed to me? I know You can, and I beg You to do so. *I implore You, cast Your eyes upon a multitude of little souls; choose from this world, I beg of You, a legion of little victims worthy of Your LOVE.*

EPILOGUE

"WE must share His sufferings if we are to share His Glory" (*Rom.* 8:17)* says St. Paul, and the degree of St. Thérèse's glory now is the measure of what she suffered on earth. It is certain that she suffered; the value of her autobiography lies in the revelation of *how* she suffered.

She had offered herself as a victim of love, but to live out this oblation in her daily life involved the suffering of walking straight along a path made crooked by the Fall. Her attitude is revealed in the following words: "Why fear to offer yourself as a victim to the merciful love of God? You might have reason to fear if it were to His divine justice, but the merciful love will have pity on your weaknesses and treat you tenderly."

It cost her dearly to leave her family; it cost as much to live in Carmel with her sisters and yet see them only when the Rule permitted. Instead, to grow in charity, she sought the company of those about her whom she found naturally the least attractive. Even when brought by her duties into more frequent

---

* Bible quotations in the Epilogue are from the translation by Msgr. Knox.

contact with Mother Agnes of Jesus, she allowed herself no useless conversations. "How I suffered then, dear Mother; I could not open my heart to you, and it was as though you knew me no longer."

Perhaps her constant struggle with her own inner self was the occasion of her greatest suffering; the effort to live independently of the demands of a nature prone to pride and impetuosity must have cost her dearly.

St. Thérèse's obedience was never influenced by personal preferences. Once, toward the end, when she had managed to be present at a community exercise but was so exhausted that she had to sit down, at a sign from one of the Sisters, she rose up and remained standing until the end.

On another occasion, when on the advice of the infirmarian she was walking in the garden, she admitted that a rest would have done her more good, but revealed what it was that gave her the strength to obey: "I offer every step for some missionary who, far away, is exhausted by his work for souls; I offer my exhaustion to relieve his."

Her self-command was so great that she could find happiness in bearing the uncharitableness of others with only a smile for answer. She never made excuses and never complained. She observed the Rule, without any dispensation, from her entry until her illness—when she was not allowed to fast—acting on the principle that we should go to the end of our strength before complaining. Such was her indifference in the matter of food that those who sat near her could never find out what she preferred. She admitted later that her practice of taking whatever was set before her involved many a mortification.

St. Thérèse found many of the practices of the Rule repugnant, yet she never relaxed her absolute obedience even to the observance of the most minute recommendations of authority. "*He who is faithful in that which is least, is faithful also in that which is greater.*" (*Luke* 16:10). It was this faithfulness in small things which led her to sanctity as exemplar of the "Little Way."

Mortifications over and above those which came her way in the normal exercise of her duties were not for her. Early in her spiritual life, she did for a time wear a little cross with small iron points which bit into her flesh. This caused her to be ill. "A small thing like this would not have had such an effect had God not willed to teach me that the great austerities practiced by some of the Saints are not for me or for those 'little souls' who are to walk the path of spiritual childhood."

The winters of Normandy are long and the climate of Lisieux is damp; there was no fire save for a few moments each day; bitterly cold all day, she spent her nights often enough awake and shivering. "Throughout my religious life," St. Thérèse revealed at the end, "the cold has caused me more physical pain than anything else; I suffered from cold until I nearly died." She admitted, however, that such suffering should be guarded against in the observance of the Rule, as a counsel of prudence.

On April 3, 1896, Good Friday, she had her first hemorrhage. Making light of it to her Superiors, she went on as usual.

Her true state was not revealed until May, and in the meantime nothing was done to relieve it. "Dear Little Mother," she said to Mother Agnes, "thank God I never told you, for it would have pained your heart had you known and seen how little was done for me."

She was given a stronger diet and for a while seemed better; she even prayed that she might recover sufficiently to join the Carmelite community of Hanoi, who had asked for her. Because of her fortitude she was allowed to continue her community duties, but so great was her exhaustion that, on reaching her cell at night, it took her an hour to undress before spending a night of pain; yet she refused aid. "I am only too glad," she would say, "to be in a cell where I cannot be heard by the Sisters, and can suffer alone; my happiness goes when I am offered sympathy and attention."

Her heroic virtue was exercised in such ordinary ways that it was not easily recognizable. One Sister was heard to remark: "She is very good, but she has certainly never done anything worth speaking about." St. Thérèse herself, however, had long ago learned to be quite indifferent to the opinion of others in such matters and sought only to please Christ.

Likening her life to a glass of medicine, beautiful to behold but bitter to taste, she went on to say that this bitterness had not made her life sad because she had learned to find joy and sweetness in bitter things.

"It has come to this," she said, "that I can no longer suffer because all suffering is sweet."

She did not dwell upon the painful aspects of her oblation nor think of what she might yet have to bear. "We who move in the way of Love must never allow ourselves to be disquieted by anything. If I did not suffer simply from moment to moment, I would find it impossible to be patient, but I look only at the present, forget the past and am careful never to anticipate the future. When we surrender to discouragment or despair, it is usually because we are thinking too much of the past or the future. Nevertheless, do pray for me; when I call out for help from Heaven, it is then, often enough, that I feel most abandoned."

Her novices asked her what she did when she experienced this sense of being abandoned.

"I turn to God and the Saints, and in spite of this feeling, I thank them, for I am sure they only want to see how far I am going to trust them. I have really taken to heart the words of Job, '*Even if God should kill me, I would still trust in Him.*' (*Job* 13:15). It has, I confess, taken me a long time to reach such self-surrender; I have reached it, yet it was Jesus Himself who brought me there.

"My heart is filled to the brim with the Will of Our Lord, so that nothing else can find place there, but glides across like oil over tranquil waters.

"If my heart were not already full and room were left for passing feelings of joy and sadness, then bitterness would flood in, but such transitory feelings scarcely ruffle the surface of my soul; a peace that nothing can disturb reigns in its depths."

Despite the lack of sensible joy over the closeness

of Heaven, she pursued her way of complete confidence and abandonment to the Will of Christ.

"I desire neither death nor life. I would not choose even if Our Lord were to give me the choice. I will only what He wills, and it is what He does that pleases me. I do not fear the last struggle nor any pain involved in my illness, however severe."

"God has always helped me, leading me by the hand since my childhood, and I rely upon Him now. Though I should endure the extremity of suffering, I know He will be there with me."

There was one night when this confidence was really put to the test. A voice seemed to come from the darkness of her anguish. "Are you sure God loves you? Has He Himself ever told you He does? You are not justified before Him on the opinion of a few mortals."

She earnestly begged prayers as her suffering increased and asked that her bed be sprinkled with holy water.

A note from her sister, reminding her of the past graces by which Christ had proved His love, set her heart at rest.

Another night she experienced the presence of the devil. "I do not see him, but I do feel him near me. He crucifies me in a grip of iron to deprive me of all consolation, trying, by increasing my sufferings, to make me despair."

"I cannot pray; only look at Our Lady; only say 'Jesus.'"

"Something mysterious is going on inside me, I am suffering for someone else, not just for myself, and Satan is aroused."

As she had found relief before through the use of holy water, so now a blessed candle dispelled the evil presence.

Until confined to her bed, even after nights spent in extreme pain, she had dragged herself to the grille, counting no sacrifice too great to receive Christ, but from August 16 till September 30, when she died, Communion was impossible owing to frequent bouts of sickness.

In April, 1895, she had told one of the older nuns that she would soon die, though she was then in good health. "I do not say it will be a matter of months, but at most within two or three years."

She was also conscious that her union with Christ was to bear fruit in eternity, and this was no lack of humility; it was a simple recognition of the graces already bestowed upon her.

"I have given nothing but love to God and He will repay with love. After my death I will let fall a shower of roses." To her, the happiness of Heaven was "to love and be loved and come back to earth to win love for our Love." She thought only of the love she would soon be able to give and receive. On July 17, 1897, she said: "I feel that my mission is soon to begin, to make others love God as I do, to teach others my 'little way.' I will spend my Heaven in doing good upon earth. Why not, since the Angels can take care of us while still enjoying the Beatific Vision? I will not be able to rest until the end of the world when the Angel has said: '*Time is no more!*' (*Apoc.* 10:6). Then I shall rest and be able to rejoice, for the number of the elect will be complete."

When questioned on what she meant by her "Little Way," she told Mother Agnes: "It is the way of spiritual childhood, the way of trust and complete self-surrender. I want to teach others the means I have always found so completely successful, to let them know that the only thing to do on earth is to offer Our Lord the flowers of little sacrifices and win Him by our proofs of love. It is the way I have won Him and why I shall find such a welcome."

She told her novices that if she found she was wrong about her "Little Way" she would make sure they ceased to follow it. "I would come back to earth at once and tell you to go another way. If I do not come back, then believe that this is true: 'We can never have too much confidence in our God, who is so mighty and merciful. As we hope in Him so shall we receive.'" On January 16, 1910, she appeared to the Prioress of the Carmelite Convent of Gallipoli in Italy and told her: "My way is sure and I was not misguided in following it."

St. Thérèse would never desire favors out of the ordinary. "In my 'little way,'" she said, "everything is most ordinary; everything I do must be within the reach of other little souls also."

She acquired the habit of greeting painful and repugnant things with a smile. "I have always forced myself to love suffering and to welcome it joyfully." "Little crosses give me more joy than anything else." "Can a victim of love find anything her Spouse sends terrible?" "Every moment He sends what I can bear and no more; He increases my strength to meet my pain. I am too little to ask for greater suffering; having chosen it myself, I should have to bear it myself, and I have never been able to do anything by myself."

In these dispositions she was able to endure the intense sufferings of her last days without losing patience and even with supernatural joy. "My sufferings are very intense indeed, yet nevertheless I am extraordinarily at peace. All my desires are realized and I am full of confidence."

One night the infirmarian found her awake, gazing toward Heaven. "What are you doing? You ought to be trying to sleep."

"I can't, Sister, I am suffering too much for that, so I pray."

"What do you say to Jesus?"

"Nothing, I just love Him."

She even found in her suffering a proof of God's goodness. "How very good God must be," she said, "to give me strength to bear all I endure."

She was fully prepared for whatever form her last agony might take: "If at the last I suffer greatly, with no indication of peace, do not worry, Mother; Our Lord Himself surely died a victim to love, yet who can measure His agony?" The day before she died she told her sister Céline, "Love alone counts."

At half past two on September 30, she told Mother Agnes, "The chalice, Mother, is full to overflowing. I could not have believed one could bear so much and can explain it only by my great desire to save souls. Thy will be done, my God, but have mercy on me; sweet Virgin Mary, aid me."

She went on to say: "All I have written about my thirst for suffering is quite true; I do not regret surrendering myself to Love."

At a few moments past seven, when she knew the end had come, she said calmly, "I do not wish to suffer less. Oh, how I love Him! My God, I love Thee." Gazing beyond the statue of Mary beside her bed, her eyes alight with a supernatural joy, she died.

Since then St. Thérèse has indeed been spending her Heaven doing good on earth: *"A grain of wheat must fall into the ground and die, but if it dies, then it yields rich fruit."* (*John* 12:25).

If you have enjoyed this book, consider making your next selection from among the following . . .

The Guardian Angels. 2.00
Eucharistic Miracles. *Joan Carroll Cruz*. 15.00
The Incorruptibles. *Joan Carroll Cruz* 13.50
Padre Pio—The Stigmatist. *Fr. Charles Carty* 15.00
Ven. Francisco Marto of Fatima. *Cirrincione,* comp.. . . . . 1.50
The Facts About Luther. *Msgr. P. O'Hare* 16.50
Little Catechism of the Curé of Ars. *St. John Vianney*. 6.00
The Curé of Ars—Patron St. of Parish Priests. *O'Brien* 5.50
The Four Last Things: Death, Judgment, Hell, Heaven 7.00
Pope St. Pius X. *F. A. Forbes* 8.00
St. Alphonsus Liguori. *Frs. Miller & Aubin* 16.50
Confession of a Roman Catholic. *Paul Whitcomb*. 1.50
The Catholic Church Has the Answer. *Paul Whitcomb* 1.50
The Sinner's Guide. *Ven. Louis of Granada* 12.00
True Devotion to Mary. *St. Louis De Montfort* 7.00
Life of St. Anthony Mary Claret. *Fanchón Royer* 15.00
Autobiography of St. Anthony Mary Claret 13.00
I Wait for You. *Sr. Josefa Menendez* .75
Words of Love. *Menendez, Betrone, Mary of the Trinity* 6.00
Little Lives of the Great Saints. *John O'Kane Murray* 18.00
Prayer—The Key to Salvation. *Fr. Michael Müller*. 7.50
The Victories of the Martyrs. *St. Alphonsus Liguori* 10.00
Canons and Decrees of the Council of Trent. *Schroeder* 15.00
Sermons of St. Alphonsus Liguori for Every Sunday 16.50
A Catechism of Modernism. *Fr. J. B. Lemius* 5.00
Alexandrina—The Agony and the Glory. *Johnston* 6.00
Life of Blessed Margaret of Castello. *Fr. Bonniwell* 7.50
The Ways of Mental Prayer. *Dom Vitalis Lehodey* 14.00
Fr. Paul of Moll. *van Speybrouck* 11.00
Abortion: Yes or No? *Dr. John L. Grady, M.D.* 2.00
The Story of the Church. *Johnson, Hannan, Dominica* 16.50
Hell Quizzes. *Radio Replies Press* 1.00
Purgatory Quizzes. *Radio Replies Press* 1.00
Virgin and Statue Worship Quizzes. *Radio Replies Press* 1.00
The Holy Eucharist. *St. Alphonsus* 10.00
Meditation Prayer on Mary Immaculate. *Padre Pio* 1.25
Little Book of the Work of Infinite Love. *de la Touche* 2.00
Textual Concordance of/Holy Scriptures. *Williams.* H.B. 35.00
Douay-Rheims Bible. *Leatherbound* 35.00
The Way of Divine Love. (pocket, unabr.). *Menendez*. 8.50
Mystical City of God—Abridged. *Ven. Mary of Agreda* 18.50

Prices subject to change.

Stories of Padre Pio. *Tangari* 8.00
Miraculous Images of Our Lady. *Joan Carroll Cruz* 20.00
Miraculous Images of Our Lord. *Cruz* 13.50
Brief Catechism for Adults. *Fr. Cogan* 9.00
Raised from the Dead. *Fr. Hebert* 16.50
Autobiography of St. Margaret Mary 5.00
Thoughts and Sayings of St. Margaret Mary 5.00
The Voice of the Saints. *Comp. by Francis Johnston* 6.00
The 12 Steps to Holiness and Salvation. *St. Alphonsus* 7.50
The Rosary and the Crisis of Faith. *Cirrincione/Nelson* 2.00
Sin and Its Consequences. *Cardinal Manning* 6.00
Fourfold Sovereignty of God. *Cardinal Manning* 5.00
Dialogue of St. Catherine of Siena. *Transl. Thorold* 10.00
Catholic Answer to Jehovah's Witnesses. *D'Angelo* 10.00
Twelve Promises of the Sacred Heart. (100 cards) 5.00
Life of St. Aloysius Gonzaga. *Fr. Meschler* 12.00
The Love of Mary. *D. Roberto* 8.00
Begone Satan. *Fr. Vogl* 3.00
The Prophets and Our Times. *Fr. R. G. Culleton* 12.50
St. Therese, The Little Flower. *John Beevers* 6.00
Mary, The Second Eve. *Cardinal Newman* 2.50
Devotion to Infant Jesus of Prague. *Booklet* .... .75
The Wonder of Guadalupe. *Francis Johnston* 7.50
Apologetics. *Msgr. Paul Glenn* 10.00
Baltimore Catechism No. 1 .... 3.50
Baltimore Catechism No. 2 .... 4.50
Baltimore Catechism No. 3 .... 8.00
An Explanation of the Baltimore Catechism. *Kinkead* 16.50
Bible History. *Schuster* 10.00
Blessed Eucharist. *Fr. Mueller* 9.00
Catholic Catechism. *Fr. Faerber* 7.00
The Devil. *Fr. Delaporte* 6.00
Dogmatic Theology for the Laity. *Fr. Premm* 20.00
Evidence of Satan in the Modern World. *Cristiani* 10.00
Fifteen Promises of Mary. (100 cards) 5.00
Life of Anne Catherine Emmerich. 2 vols. *Schmoeger* 37.50
Life of the Blessed Virgin Mary. *Emmerich* 16.50
Prayer to St. Michael. (100 leaflets) 5.00
Prayerbook of Favorite Litanies. *Fr. Hebert* 10.00
Preparation for Death. (Abridged). *St. Alphonsus* 8.00
Purgatory Explained. *Schouppe* 13.50
Purgatory Explained. (pocket, unabr.). *Schouppe* 9.00
Spiritual Conferences. *Tauler* 13.00
Trustful Surrender to Divine Providence. *Bl. Claude* 5.00

Prices subject to change.

Forty Dreams of St. John Bosco. *Bosco* 12.50
Blessed Miguel Pro. *Ball* 6.00
Soul Sanctified. *Anonymous* 9.00
Wife, Mother and Mystic. *Bessieres* 8.00
The Agony of Jesus. *Padre Pio*.................... 1.50
Catholic Home Schooling. *Mary Kay Clark* 18.00
The Cath. Religion—Illus. & Expl. *Msgr. Burbach*......... 9.00
Wonders of the Holy Name. *Fr. O'Sullivan*.......... 1.50
How Christ Said the First Mass. *Fr. Meagher*............ 18.50
Too Busy for God? Think Again! *D'Angelo* 5.00
St. Bernadette Soubirous. *Trochu* 18.50
Passion and Death of Jesus Christ. *Liguori*............ 10.00
Life Everlasting. *Garrigou-Lagrange* 13.50
Confession Quizzes. *Radio Replies Press* 1.00
St. Philip Neri. *Fr. V. J. Matthews*................. 5.50
St. Louise de Marillac. *Sr. Vincent Regnault* 6.00
The Old World and America. *Rev. Philip Furlong*.......... 18.00
Prophecy for Today. *Edward Connor* 5.50
Bethlehem. *Fr. Faber* 18.00
The Book of Infinite Love. *Mother de la Touche* 5.00
The Church Teaches. *Church Documents* 16.50
Conversation with Christ. *Peter T. Rohrbach* 10.00
Purgatory and Heaven. *J. P. Arendzen*.............. 5.00
Liberalism Is a Sin. *Sarda y Salvany*................ 7.50
Spiritual Legacy/Sr. Mary of Trinity. *van den Broek*......... 10.00
The Creator and the Creature. *Fr. Frederick Faber*......... 16.50
Radio Replies. 3 Vols. *Frs. Rumble and Carty*............. 36.00
Convert's Catechism of Catholic Doctrine. *Geiermann*....... 3.00
Incarnation, Birth, Infancy of Jesus Christ. *Liguori*.......... 10.00
Light and Peace. *Fr. R. P. Quadrupani* 7.00
Dogmatic Canons & Decrees of Trent, Vat. I....... 9.50
The Evolution Hoax Exposed. *A. N. Field* 6.00
The Priest, the Man of God. *St. Joseph Cafasso* 12.50
Christ Denied. *Fr. Paul Wickens* 2.50
New Regulations on Indulgences. *Fr. Winfrid Herbst* 2.50
A Tour of the Summa. *Msgr. Paul Glenn* 18.00
Spiritual Conferences. *Fr. Frederick Faber*............ 15.00
Bible Quizzes. *Radio Replies Press* 1.00
Marriage Quizzes. *Radio Replies Press*............. 1.00
True Church Quizzes. *Radio Replies Press*........... 1.00
Mary, Mother of the Church. *Church Documents* 4.00
The Sacred Heart and the Priesthood. *de la Touche*......... 9.00
Blessed Sacrament. *Fr. Faber*..................... 18.50
Revelations of St. Bridget. *St. Bridget of Sweden* 3.00

Prices subject to change.

Story of a Soul. *St. Therese of Lisieux* 8.00
Catholic Children's Treasure Box Books 1-10 .... 35.00
Prayers and Heavenly Promises. *Cruz*. 5.00
Magnificent Prayers. *St. Bridget of Sweden* 2.00
The Happiness of Heaven. *Fr. J. Boudreau*. 8.00
The Glories of Mary. *St. Alphonsus Liguori* 16.50
The Glories of Mary. (pocket, unabr.). *St. Alphonsus* 10.00
The Curé D'Ars. *Abbé Francis Trochu* 21.50
Humility of Heart. *Fr. Cajetan da Bergamo* 8.50
Love, Peace and Joy. (St. Gertrude). *Prévot* 7.00
Père Lamy. *Biver* 10.00
Passion of Jesus & Its Hidden Meaning. *Groenings* 15.00
Mother of God & Her Glorious Feasts. *Fr. O'Laverty*. 10.00
Song of Songs—A Mystical Exposition. *Fr. Arintero* 20.00
Love and Service of God, Infinite Love. *de la Touche* 12.50
Life & Work of Mother Louise Marg. *Fr. O'Connell* 12.50
Martyrs of the Coliseum. *O'Reilly* 18.50
Rhine Flows into the Tiber. *Fr. Wiltgen*. 15.00
What Catholics Believe. *Fr. Lawrence Lovasik* 5.00
Who Is Therese Neumann? *Fr. Charles Carty*. 2.00
Summa of the Christian Life. 3 Vols. *Granada* 36.00
St. Francis of Paola. *Simi and Segreti* 8.00
The Rosary in Action. *John Johnson*. 9.00
St. Dominic. *Sr. Mary Jean Dorcy* 10.00
Is It a Saint's Name? *Fr. William Dunne* 1.50
St. Martin de Porres. *Giuliana Cavallini*. 12.50
Douay-Rheims New Testament. *Paperbound* 15.00
St. Catherine of Siena. *Alice Curtayne* 13.50
Blessed Virgin Mary. *Liguori* 4.50
Chats With Converts. *Fr. M. D. Forrest* 10.00
The Stigmata and Modern Science. *Fr. Charles Carty* 1.25
St. Gertrude the Great 1.50
Thirty Favorite Novenas .... .75
Brief Life of Christ. *Fr. Rumble* 2.00
Catechism of Mental Prayer. *Msgr. Simler* 2.00
On Freemasonry. *Pope Leo XIII* 1.50
Thoughts of the Curé D'Ars. *St. John Vianney* 2.00
Incredible Creed of Jehovah Witnesses. *Fr. Rumble* 1.00
St. Pius V—His Life, Times, Miracles. *Anderson* 5.00
St. Dominic's Family. *Sr. Mary Jean Dorcy* 24.00
St. Rose of Lima. *Sr. Alphonsus* 15.00
Latin Grammar. *Scanlon & Scanlon* 16.50
Second Latin. *Scanlon & Scanlon*. 12.00
St. Joseph of Copertino. *Pastrovicchi* 6.00

Prices subject to change.

Saint Michael and the Angels. *Approved Sources* 7.00
Dolorous Passion of Our Lord. *Anne C. Emmerich* 16.50
Our Lady of Fatima's Peace Plan from Heaven. *Booklet* 75
Three Ways of the Spiritual Life. *Garrigou-Lagrange* 6.00
Mystical Evolution. 2 Vols. *Fr. Arintero, O.P.* 33.00
St. Catherine Labouré of the Mirac. Medal. *Fr. Dirvin* 13.50
Manual of Practical Devotion to St. Joseph. *Patrignani* 15.00
The Active Catholic. *Fr. Palau* 7.00
Ven. Jacinta Marto of Fatima. *Cirrincione* 2.00
Reign of Christ the King. *Davies* 1.25
St. Teresa of Ávila. *William Thomas Walsh* 21.50
Isabella of Spain—The Last Crusader. *Wm. T. Walsh* 20.00
Characters of the Inquisition. *Wm. T. Walsh* 15.00
Philip II. *William Thomas Walsh.* H.B. 37.50
Blood-Drenched Altars—Cath. Comment. Hist. Mexico 20.00
Self-Abandonment to Divine Providence. *de Caussade* 18.00
Way of the Cross. *Liguorian* 1.00
Way of the Cross. *Franciscan* 1.00
Modern Saints—Their Lives & Faces, Bk. 1. *Ann Ball* 18.00
Modern Saints—Their Lives & Faces, Bk. 2. *Ann Ball* 20.00
Divine Favors Granted to St. Joseph. *Pere Binet* 5.00
St. Joseph Cafasso—Priest of the Gallows. *St. J. Bosco* 4.50
Catechism of the Council of Trent. *McHugh/Callan* 24.00
Why Squander Illness? *Frs. Rumble & Carty* 2.00
Fatima—The Great Sign. *Francis Johnston* 8.00
Heliotropium—Conformity of Human Will to Divine 13.00
Charity for the Suffering Souls. *Fr. John Nageleisen* 16.50
Devotion to the Sacred Heart of Jesus. *Verheylezoon* 15.00
Sermons on Prayer. *St. Francis de Sales* 4.00
Sermons on Our Lady. *St. Francis de Sales* 10.00
Sermons for Lent. *St. Francis de Sales* 12.00
Fundamentals of Catholic Dogma. *Ott* 21.00
Litany of the Blessed Virgin Mary. (100 cards) 5.00
Who Is Padre Pio? *Radio Replies Press* 1.50
Child's Bible History. *Knecht* 4.00
The Life of Christ. 4 Vols. H.B. *Anne C. Emmerich* 60.00
St. Anthony—The Wonder Worker of Padua. *Stoddard* 5.00
The Precious Blood. *Fr. Faber* 13.50
The Holy Shroud & Four Visions. *Fr. O'Connell* 2.00
Clean Love in Courtship. *Fr. Lawrence Lovasik* 2.50
The Secret of the Rosary. *St. Louis De Montfort* 3.00

At your Bookdealer or direct from the Publisher.
Call Toll Free 1-800-437-5876

Prices subject to change.